BREAD MACHINE
100 GREAT
RECIPES

BREAD MACHINE
100 GREAT RECIPES

Jacqueline Bellefontaine

SB

Published by SILVERDALE BOOKS
An imprint of Bookmart Ltd
Registered number 2372865
Trading as Bookmart Ltd
Blaby Road
Wigston
Leicester, LE18 4SE

© 2004 D&S Books Ltd

D&S Books Ltd
Kerswell,
Parkham Ash, Bideford
Devon, England
EX39 5PR

e-mail us at:-
enquiries@dsbooks.fsnet.co.uk

This edition printed 2004

ISBN 1-845090-59-4

DS0140 100 More Bread Machine Recipes

Creative Director: Sarah King
Editor: Sally MacEachern
Project editor: Sally MacEachern
Photographer: Colin Bowling/PaulForrester
Designer: Axis Design Editions Ltd

Typeset in Galliard and Helvetica

Printed in China

1 3 5 7 9 10 8 6 4 2

CONTENTS

INTRODUCTION

BREAD HAS BEEN A STAPLE PART OF OUR DIET FOR thousands of years, and now you can enjoy bread made at home with the minimum of fuss and time, thanks to the arrival of the home bread-making machine. Bread is a versatile food that can form the basis of a meal, make a tasty addition to a meal, or be used to make a healthy snack at any time of the day. Bread is an important part of our daily diet, providing us with protein, calcium, iron, Vitamin B1 (thiamine) and niacin.

Bread machines have been designed to take the hard work out of bread making.

While bread making has never been very difficult, it has been time consuming. With the help of a bread machine, bread making can be both easy and less time consuming. For a basic loaf all you need do is weigh out the

ingredients, set the timer and leave the machine to do the rest. Those of you who enjoy a more hands-on approach can leave the machine to do the hard work of kneading and making the dough, while you finish the job, baking the bread in the oven for a more traditional treat.

Bread lovers no longer have to put up with mass-produced bread or pay a small fortune for artisan bread because they can enjoy the fabulous aroma and taste of fresh baked bread at home. You can choose from traditional breads or fashionable, flavoured breads, easy-to-make breads or more challenging breads, such as sour dough. All you need is a bread machine and a handful of ingredients – you will find recipes for all of these breads in this book. In fact, I am sure, it will not be long before you wonder how you ever managed without a bread machine.

Choosing a bread machine

All bread machines work on the same basic principle and make the same basic breads (although the programme times may vary). Many will make cakes or have a bake-only programme. Some have additional programmes such as continental breads, jams and pasta. Choose a machine with programmes that will suit you. If you want to wake up to the wonderful aroma of fresh baked bread for breakfast a timer is a must. Consider also the capacity of the machine – those that make larger loaves will usually make smaller loaves, but not vice versa. Even if you think that a small loaf will be enough for you, once you have got the taste for fresh home-made bread a small loaf may just not be enough. It is also worth noting that some of the budget models have fewer programme variations and many have a limited capacity.

The majority of the recipes in this book use no more than 500g/1lb2oz dry ingredients and can be cooked in most machines. However, some recipes exceed this.

Important Note
Always check the capacity of the machine before beginning a recipe.

I have given quantities for small and larger loaves for the basic bread recipes. Once you are familiar with your machine and with making basic breads, you can use these quantities as a guide if you want to increase the size of the other breads.

For the recipes in this book I have used programmes that are universal to most bread machine models on the market.

Tips for success

The ingredients for bread making need to be used in the right proportions and under the correct conditions for success. This recipe book, in conjunction with the manufacturer's handbook and the bread machine, will help you to achieve the right results.

• Read the instruction manual to familiarise yourself with the machine and to check the capacity of the machine. Always add the ingredients in the order suggested in the manual. Some machines require the wet ingredients to be added first, others require the dry ingredients first. Whichever method your machine requires it is important to ensure that the yeast does not come into contact with the liquid, especially in machines that do not start mixing immediately, or when using the timer.

• As with all baking, accurate measuring is essential. For the greatest accuracy I like to use electronic scales but any good scales will do. The advantage of electronic scales is that they save on washing up. You can place the bread pan directly on the scales and weigh the ingredients in the pan, zeroing the scales between each ingredient. Even the water can be weighed – 1ml = 1g water/1fl oz–1oz water. (This is not true of all liquids.) You may find that the cup often supplied with the machine is more convenient than a conventional measuring jug. The cup has more graduations, which makes it easier to measure accurately.

• For spoon measurements always use measuring spoons. Many manufacturers supply a measuring spoon with the machine.

• Unless otherwise stated, ingredients should always be at room temperature. Water can be added straight from the tap unless it is very cold.

• While the machine goes a long way towards providing the correct conditions for bread making, the results can be affected by outside factors, such as humidity and room temperature. It is a good idea to check the consistency of the dough during kneading. The dough should form a smooth ball that is slightly springy to the touch. If the dough is too wet, add a little extra flour, a tablespoon at a time. If it is too dry, add extra water, a tablespoon at a time. If some of the ingredients have stuck to the sides of the pan use a rubber spatula to scrape down the sides. While it is not essential to do this (nor is it practical if using the timer overnight), it is worth doing when you can – especially the first few times you use the machine – to ensure good results.

• Additional ingredients, such as nuts or fruit, are added towards the end of the kneading, so that they are not broken up too much during the process. Most machines will bleep to let you know when to add them. Some machines even have a special compartment that will add the ingredients automatically. If your machine does not have either of these facilities, add the ingredients about 5 minutes before the end of kneading (see instruction manual for chart of programme times to gauge when this will be).

• Never use perishable ingredients that should be refrigerated, such as milk, cream, buttermilk and eggs, when using the timer as they may spoil. Dried milk powder can be used.

• If the paddle sticks in the bread when it is removed from the pan, allow the loaf to cool before removing it.

The ingredients

FLOUR

Flour is the principal ingredient used in bread making. When making bread it is essential that you use a flour labelled "strong" or "bread" flour. These flours have a high gluten content, and it is this that forms the texture and structure of breads. Plain or self-raising flour has a lower gluten content and will not work.

Wholemeal flour is made by milling the entire wheat kernel, and it includes the bran and germ. Brown flour has 10 to 15 percent of the wheat grain removed during milling. Both produce a denser and smaller loaf than those made with white flour. This is because the gluten strands are cut by the edges of the bran

Weighing flour using electronic scales.

flakes and germ. Wholemeal flours are also rich in minerals, which inhibit the fermentation of the yeast.

Other flours, such as rye, spelt and buckwheat, which have a low gluten content, can be added to bread for a different flavour and texture but must be used in small quantities with a strong bread flour. Flour is best stored in a cool, dry, dark place.

LIQUIDS

Water is the liquid most commonly used in bread making although milk, fruit juice and beer can also be used to add flavour. Use liquids at room temperature. Warm them slightly if using straight from the fridge. Milk not only adds nutritional value to the bread, it also improves its keeping quality and the colour of the crust. For this reason, milk powder is often added to recipes. If you do not wish to add milk powder where specified, it can be omitted but the bread may not keep as long. Skimmed, semi-skimmed or full-fat milk may be used. Always measure liquids carefully and do not use fresh milk if using the timer.

Carefully measure and add water to the pan.

YEAST

Yeast is the raising agent used in bread. It is a living organism, and once activated it creates carbon dioxide, small bubbles of which become trapped within the gluten-rich structure of the dough, giving the bread its characteristic texture.

Yeast is available in fresh and dried forms. Dried yeast comes in two types: one that requires preliminary fermentation, and another that is used dry and may be mixed with other ingredients. It is the latter that is used in bread machines. This yeast is sometimes called easy blend, easy bake, fast action, or instant dried yeast. They are all the same, but with different marketing names. Most manufacturers now label them as suitable for use in bread machines to avoid confusion. They are often sold in sachets. Once opened, the sachets should be resealed and used within 48 hours. If you make a lot of bread, you can buy larger packets, which will keep for up to three months in the refrigerator.

Yeast works quickest in warm conditions, which are conveniently supplied by the bread machine. It will also work at low temperatures but much more slowly – the dough can be made, shaped and left to rise overnight in the refrigerator. Allow the dough to return to room temperature before baking. Too high a temperature will kill yeast.

SALT

Salt is an essential ingredient that is not only used for flavour, but also controls the growth of yeast and strengthens gluten structure. Too much salt will inhibit fermentation and too little will result in a poor gluten structure – both will result in a poor loaf with low volume. Do not adjust the amount in the recipes as it may affect the finished product.

SUGAR

Sugar speeds up the action of the yeast, as well as affecting the keeping quality of the bread by helping to retain moisture. My preferred choice is either caster sugar (I like to use golden caster, which is a less refined sugar) or light muscovado sugar for added flavour. However, most sugars can be used.

Honey can also be used for flavour. Bread with a high sugar content will have a darker crust when baked, so select the light crust setting for sweet breads, if a choice is available.

Sugar absorbs moisture from the air. As it dries out again it can become hard and lumpy – a particular problem with brown sugars. A piece of bread in the storage container with the sugar will absorb the moisture from the air and help to prevent the sugar from going hard.

FATS AND OILS

Fats and oils tenderise bread, add flavour and richness and contribute to the keeping qualities. Any fat or oil can be used. I generally like to use olive oil or butter, depending on the flavour required. Butter and other fats must be softened and at room temperature before being added.

FLAVOURINGS

Other ingredients are added to bread to change the flavour and/or texture. The most commonly used flavourings include:

Eggs – They give a rich flavour and a more cakey texture. Eggs used in these recipes are medium. Add at room temperature. Do not use eggs when using the timer.

Fruit and vegetables – Fresh or dried fruit and vegetables add flavour and variety. Fresh fruit and vegetables will affect the water content of the bread so use only as directed in the recipe.

Nuts – Chop finely and use no more than the recipes recommend. Chopped nuts may reduce the volume of breads as they will cut the gluten fibres.

Seeds, herbs and spices – Add flavour and/or texture.

DOUGH ENHANCER

A dough enhancer is available from some specialist stores and by mail order from Lakeland Limited (015394 88100). It consists of a blend of vital wheat gluten, diastic malt and ascorbic acid (vitamin C). Dough enhancer can be added to breads with high wholemeal content or to flours with low gluten content to improve the structure. It can be omitted from the recipes but a denser loaf will result.

16

Slicing and Storing Bread

Remove the bread from the pan as soon as possible after baking and place it on a wire rack to cool. This will prevent the bread from sweating in the tin and getting a soggy crust. Most bread machines have a keep-warm facility to help prevent this from happening, if you are not available immediately.

Important Note

REMEMBER ALWAYS TO USE OVEN GLOVES WHEN REMOVING THE PAN AND TURNING OUT THE BREAD. THE BREAD AND PAN WILL BE HOT.

Allow the bread to cool before slicing it as cutting bread fresh from the oven may be difficult.

To store bread, allow it to cool completely at room temperature and then wrap it in foil or a plastic bag. If well covered, bread will last for up to three days. However, for the best flavour, try to consume your bread as soon as possible. Do not store bread in the refrigerator, as it will dry out. Bread can be frozen. Many of the breads in this book make delicious toast.

Trouble Shooting

If you find that the loaf is not as perfect as you had hoped, do not despair. Remember there is a certain charm to the variations that occur in home-made bread. While your bread might not always look prefect and its colour or texture may vary, more often than not it will still be delicious to eat.

You may encounter the following problems while using the bread machine:

The bread did not rise enough.
Too little yeast.
Too little sugar.
Too much salt, or the yeast has come into contact with the salt before mixing.
Yeast activated too soon by being in contact with the liquids.
The yeast is out of date.

The bread has sunk in the centre.
Too much liquid.
No salt or too little salt.
Too much yeast.

The crust is damp and has lost its crunch.

Loaf left in the tin too long before turning out to cool on a rack.

Loaf wrapped while still warm.

The centre is soggy or uncooked.

Too much liquid, or too many "wet" ingredients.

Too many rich ingredients, such as nuts or other grains.

The bread rises too much.

Too much yeast.

Too little salt.

The crust is over browned.

Too much sugar

Choose a light crust setting for sweet breads.

Texture is too dense.

Not enough liquid.

STRAIGHT FROM THE PAN

The recipes in this section of the book require you simply to measure the ingredients, set the programmes and leave the machine to do the hard work. Start with the basic breads to familiarise yourself with the machine. You will soon move on to make interesting and tasty variations. There are plenty of variations to choose from in both the sweet and savoury sections.

If you like, you can glaze bread before the baking cycle begins. For a crisp, shiny finish brush the top with a little beaten egg. Try sprinkling some seeds, oat wheat or rye flakes on the bread before baking for a more visually interesting loaf. Work quickly and close the lid as soon as possible to prevent too much heat from escaping. Sweet breads can be finished after cooking with a sweet sugar and water glaze, a brushing of honey or sieved apricot jam. Savoury breads can be brushed with melted butter for a rich soft crust.

Basic White Loaf

This is a good recipe to start with and to familiarise yourself with your machine's settings. It will be sure to become a regular as you discover just how easy making your own bread in a bread machine is. You may never buy a bought loaf again!

Remove the bread pan from the machine. Pour in the water. Add the butter, sugar and salt. Now add the

Small Loaf:
240ml/8½fl oz water
25g/1oz butter
1 tbsp sugar
1 tsp salt
450g/1lb strong white
  bread flour
1½ tbsp milk powder
  (optional)
1 tsp fast acting dried yeast

Large Loaf:
350ml/12fl oz water
40g/1½oz butter
2 tbsp sugar
1½ tsp salt
600g/1lb 6oz strong white
  bread flour
2 tbsp dried milk powder
  (optional)
1½ tsp fast acting dried yeast

Adding flour.

flour, making sure you cover the water. Place the milk powder, if using, in one corner. Sprinkle the yeast over the flour. If your machine recommends that you add the dry ingredients first, simply reverse the order that you add them to the pan.

Fit the bread pan in the machine, set the programme to the basic setting, medium crust, and press start.

When the cycle is complete, switch off the machine. Using oven gloves, carefully remove the pan. Turn out the bread onto a wire rack to cool.

Milk Bread

Adding sugar.

Milk bread keeps well. In fact, milk powder is often added to bread to improve its keeping quality. The dough can be used to make more fancy, shaped bread but here it is cooked in the bread machine for ease. It makes fabulous, slightly nutty, crisp toast.

Remove the bread pan from the machine. Pour in the milk. Add the butter, sugar and salt. Add the flour, making sure that the milk is completely covered. Sprinkle the yeast over the flour. If your machine

Small Loaf:
240ml/8½fl oz milk
25g/1oz butter
1 tbsp caster sugar
1 tsp salt
450g/1lb strong white
  bread flour
1 tsp fast-acting dried yeast

Large Loaf:
300ml/10fl oz milk
40g/1½oz butter
2 tbsp caster sugar
1½ tsp salt
600g/1lb 6oz strong white
  bread flour
1½ tsp fast-acting dried yeast

To complete:
beaten egg or milk, or
  melted butter to glaze

Working quickly, brush the top of the dough with beaten egg.

recommends that you add the dry ingredients first, simply reverse the order that you add them to the pan.

Fit the bread pan in the machine, set the programme to the basic setting, medium crust, and press start.

Just before the baking starts brush the top with beaten egg or milk to glaze. Alternatively brush a little melted butter onto the top crust when cooked.

When the cycle is complete, switch off the machine. Using oven gloves, carefully remove the pan. Turn out the bread onto a wire rack to cool.

Brown Bread

Brown flour.

Milk powder.

Brown flour has had 10–15 percent of the wheat grain removed during milling. It produces a lighter loaf than wholemeal with some of the fibre retained. I particularly like the texture of bread made with a coarse brown flour but any brown flour will work.

Remove the bread pan from the machine. Pour in the water. Add the butter, sugar and salt. Add the flour, making sure that the water is completely covered. Place the milk powder in one corner. Sprinkle the yeast over the flour. If your machine recommends that you add the dry ingredients first, simply reverse the order that you add them to the pan.

Fit the bread pan in the machine, set the programme to the wholemeal setting, medium crust, and press start.

When the cycle is complete, switch off the machine. Using oven gloves, carefully remove the pan. Turn out the bread onto a wire rack to cool.

Small Loaf:
275ml/9½fl oz water
25g/1oz butter
1 tbsp sugar
1 tsp salt
450g/1lb strong
   brown bread flour
2 tbsp dried milk powder
1 tsp fast-acting dried yeast

Large Loaf:
375ml/13fl oz water
40g/1½oz butter
2 tbsp sugar
1½ tsp salt
600g/1lb 6oz strong
   brown bread flour
2 tbsp dried milk powder
1 tsp fast-acting dried yeast

Granary Bread

Flour

Adding the yeast.

Small Loaf:
275ml/9½fl oz water
25g/1oz butter
1 tbsp caster sugar
1 tsp salt
450g/1lb granary flour
1 tbsp dried milk powder
1 tsp fast-acting dried yeast

Large Loaf:
325ml/11fl oz water
40g/1½oz butter
2 tbsp caster sugar
1½ tsp salt
600g/1lb 6oz granary flour
2 tbsp dried milk powder
1½ tsp fast-acting dried yeast

Granary flour is a combination of wholemeal, white and rye flour mixed with malted wheat grains. This makes a popular brown loaf with a sweet, nutty taste. It is lighter in texture than a wholemeal loaf and some brown breads.

Remove the bread pan from the machine. Pour in the water. Add the butter, sugar and salt. Add the flour, making sure that the water is completely covered. Place the milk powder in one corner. Sprinkle the yeast over the flour. If your machine recommends that you add the dry ingredients first, simply reverse the order that you add them to the pan.

Fit the bread pan in the machine, set the programme to the basic setting, medium crust, and press start.

When the cycle is complete, switch off the machine. Using oven gloves, carefully remove the pan. Turn out the bread onto a wire rack to cool.

Wholemeal Bread

Flour.

Vitamin C helps the gluten to develop. Adding lemon juice to wholemeal bread adds vitamin C and will help to improve the texture of the bread.

Remove the bread pan from the machine. Pour in the water. Add the lemon juice, butter, sugar and salt. Add the flour, making sure that the water is completely covered. Place the milk powder in one corner. Sprinkle the yeast over the flour. If your machine recommends that you add the dry ingredients first, simply reverse the order that you add them to the pan.

Fit the bread pan in the machine,

Small Loaf

300ml/10fl oz water
1 tbsp lemon juice
25g/1oz butter
1½ tbsp sugar
1½ tsp salt
450g/1lb strong
   wholemeal bread flour
2 tbsp dried milk powder
1¼ tsp fast-acting dried yeast

Large Loaf:

400ml/14fl oz water
1 tbsp lemon juice
40g/1½oz butter
2 tbsp sugar
1 tsp salt
600g/1lb 6oz strong
   wholemeal bread flour
2 tbsp dried milk powder
1½ tsp fast-acting dried yeast

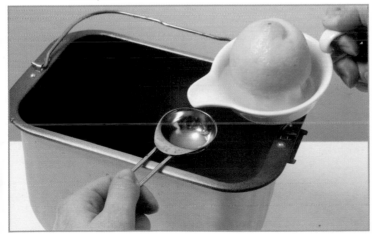

Lemon juice.

set the programme to the wholemeal setting, medium crust, and press start.

When the cycle is complete, switch off the machine. Using oven gloves, carefully remove the pan. Turn out the bread onto a wire rack to cool.

Wheatmeal Bread

I find wholemeal bread too dense and prefer wheatmeal bread, which is made from 50 percent wholemeal and 50 percent white flour. It retains some of the nutty flavour of wholemeal bread but has a lighter texture. Choose extra strong white bread flour, if available, as this has extra gluten that will help further with the rise and texture of the bread.

Remove the bread pan from the machine. Pour in the water. Add the butter, sugar and salt. Add the flour, making sure that the water is completely covered. Place the milk powder in one corner. Sprinkle the yeast over the flour. If your machine recommends that you add the dry ingredients first, simply reverse the order that you add them to the pan.

Fit the bread pan in the machine, set the programme to the wholemeal setting, medium crust, and press start.

Adding sugar.

Adding wholemeal flour.

Small Loaf:
300ml/10fl oz water
25g/1oz butter
1½ tbsp sugar
1½ tsp salt
225g/8oz strong
   wholemeal bread flour
225g/8oz extra strong
   white bread flour
2 tbsp dried milk powder
1¼ tsp fast-acting dried yeast

Large Loaf:
400ml/14fl oz water
40g/1½oz butter
2 tbsp sugar
1½ tsp salt
300g/10oz strong
   wholemeal bread flour
300g/10oz extra strong
   white bread flour
2 tbsp dried milk powder
1½ tsp fast-acting dried yeast

When the cycle is complete, switch off the machine. Using oven gloves carefully remove the pan. Turn out the bread onto a wire rack to cool.

Sunflower and Spelt Bread

Adding sunflower seeds.

Adding spelt flour.

Ingredients

300ml/10fl oz water
2 tbsp sunflower oil
1 tbsp sugar
1½ tsp salt
225g/8oz strong white
    bread flour
225g/8oz spelt flour
2 tbsp milk powder
1 tsp fast-acting dried yeast
75g/3oz sunflower seeds

Spelt is an ancestor of our modern wheat grain. It is more easily digestible than the modern wheat variety.

Remove the bread pan from the machine. Pour in the water and oil. Add the sugar and salt. Add the two flours, making sure to cover the water. Place the milk powder in one corner and sprinkle the yeast over the flour. If your machine recommends that you add the dry ingredients first, simply reverse the order that you add them to the pan.

Fit the bread pan in the machine, set the programme to the basic setting, medium crust, and press start. When the machine beeps for extra ingredients, or about 5 minutes before the end of kneading, add the sunflower seeds to the pan.

When the cycle is complete, switch off the machine. Using oven gloves, carefully remove the pan. Turn out the bread onto a wire rack to cool.

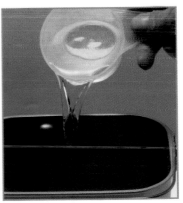

Pour the water into the pan.

Onion, Garlic and Rosemary Bread

set the programme to the basic setting, medium crust, and press start.

When the cycle is complete, switch off the machine. Using oven gloves, carefully remove the pan. Turn out the bread onto a wire rack to cool.

Rosemary.

Heat the oil in a small frying pan and sauté the onion for 3 to 4 minutes until softened. Stir in the garlic and sugar, and continue to cook for 1 to 2 minutes until the onion is just golden. Stir in the rosemary and remove from the heat.

Remove the bread pan from the machine. Pour in the water. Add the onion mixture and salt. Add the flour, making sure to cover the water. Sprinkle the yeast over the flour. If your machine recommends that you add the dry ingredients first, simply reverse the order that you add them to the pan.

Fit the bread pan in the machine,

Ingredients
2 tbsp olive oil
1 small onion, chopped
2 cloves garlic, chopped
2 tsp light muscovado sugar
1 tbsp chopped fresh
  rosemary
240ml/8½fl oz water
1½ tsp salt
450g/1lb strong white
  bread flour
1 tsp fast-acting dried yeast

Adding onion and rosemary mixture.

Cheesy Ploughman's

Adding ale.

Serve with chunks of cheese, tomato and pickle for a flavour-packed ploughman's lunch.

Remove the bread pan from the machine. Pour in the ale and water. Add the butter, sugar, salt, cheese and spring onions. Add the flours, making sure that the liquid is completely covered. Sprinkle the yeast over the flour. If your machine recommends that you add the dry

Ingredients

225ml/8fl oz pale ale
50ml/2fl oz water
25g/1oz butter
1 tbsp sugar
1 tsp salt
75g/3oz cheddar cheese, grated
6 spring onions, sliced
200g/7oz strong white bread flour
250g/9oz strong wholemeal bread flour
1 tsp fast-acting dried yeast

ingredients first, simply reverse the order that you add them to the pan.

Fit the bread pan in the machine, set the programme to the wholemeal setting, medium crust, and press start.

When the cycle is complete, switch off the machine. Using oven gloves, carefully remove the pan. Turn out the bread onto a wire rack to cool.

Grate the cheese.

41

Oat Bread

Adding oats

caption in this space

Ingredients
300ml/10fl oz milk
50ml/2fl oz water
25g/1oz butter
1 tbsp dark muscovado
　　sugar
1½ tsp salt
300g/10oz strong white
　　bread flour
150g/5oz rolled oats
1 tsp fast-acting dried yeast

To complete (optional):
a little milk for brushing
oats to sprinkle

Oats have been added to bread for centuries. They add flavour and texture to the finished bread. This loaf has a dense, moist crumb and crisp crust.

Remove the bread pan from the machine. Pour in the milk and water. Add the butter, sugar and salt. Add the flour and oats, making sure that the liquid is completely covered. Sprinkle the yeast over the flour. If your machine recommends that you add the dry ingredients first, simply reverse the order that you add them to the pan.

Fit the bread pan in the machine, set the programme to the basic setting, medium crust, and press start.

If desired, just before the baking cycle starts quickly open the lid. Brush the top with a little milk, sprinkle over a few oats and close the lid.

When the cycle is complete, switch off the machine. Using oven gloves, carefully remove the pan. Turn out the bread onto a wire rack to cool.

Italian Polenta Bread

This rustic bread is great with hearty stews and strong Italian cheeses.

Remove the bread pan from the machine. Pour in the water and oil. Add the sugar and salt. Add the flour and polenta, making sure that the water is completely covered. Sprinkle the yeast over the flour. If your machine recommends that you add the dry ingredients first, simply reverse the order that you add them to the pan.

Fit the bread pan in the machine, set the programme to the basic setting, medium crust, and press start.

When the cycle is complete, switch off the machine. Using oven gloves carefully remove the pan. Turn out the bread onto a wire rack to cool.

Ingredients
275ml/9½fl oz water
2 tbsp olive oil
1 tbsp sugar
1½ tsp salt
350g/12oz strong white bread flour
150g/5oz polenta
1 tsp fast-acting dried yeast

Adding olive oil.

Adding polenta.

Mixed Seedy Bread

Linseed

Sesame

Sunflower

Pumpkin

Selection of seeds.

Adding seeds.

Ingredients
2 tbsp linseeds
2 tbsp sesame seeds
2 tbsp sunflower seeds
2 tbsp pumpkin seeds
250ml/9fl oz water
2 tbsp sunflower oil
1 tbsp light muscovado
  sugar
1½ tsp salt
250g/9oz strong white
  bread flour
200g/7oz strong brown
  flour
1 tsp fast-acting dried yeast

This bread is packed full of flavour and has delicious crunchy bits from the seeds. It is delicious on its own, with jam or with cheese.

Lightly toast the seeds. Allow to cool.

Remove the bread pan from the machine. Pour in the water. Add the oil, sugar and salt. Add the flours, making sure that the water is completely covered. Add the seeds and sprinkle the yeast over the flour.

Tip
Toasting the seeds helps to bring out their flavour. You can do this by placing them in an oven at 180°C/350°F/gas mark 4 for 10 minutes, under a medium grill or in a dry frying pan over a low heat. If you choose the latter two methods, you will need to stir the seeds frequently and keep a very close eye on them to ensure that they do not burn.

For an attractive topping, just before the baking cycle starts, brush the bread with a little milk or beaten egg and sprinkle over some extra seeds. Work quickly so that the lid is not open for too long.

If your machine recommends that you add the dry ingredients first, simply reverse the order that you add them to the pan.

Fit the bread pan in the machine, set the programme to the basic setting, medium crust, and press start.

When the cycle is complete, switch off the machine. Using oven gloves, carefully remove the pan. Turn out the bread onto a wire rack to cool.

Multi-Grain and Seed Bread

Adding barley malt syrup.

Barley and millet flour add flavour to this dense bread, while the flour enhancer adds gluten, which is essential for the loaf to rise and hold its shape.

Remove the bread pan from the machine. Pour in the water. Add the oil, syrup and salt. Add the flours, making sure that the water is completely covered. Place the flour enhancer in one corner. Sprinkle the yeast over the flour. If your machine recommends that you add the dry ingredients first, simply reverse the order that you add them to the pan.

Fit the bread pan in the machine, set the programme to the basic setting, medium crust, and press start.

When the cycle is complete, switch off the machine. Using oven gloves, carefully remove the pan. Turn out the bread onto a wire rack to cool.

Ingredients

250ml/9fl oz water
2 tbsp sunflower oil
2 tbsp barley malt syrup
1½ tsp salt
250g/9oz strong brown bread flour
100g/4oz barley flour
100g/4oz millet flour
1 tbsp dough enhancer (see page 16)
1½tsp fast-acting dried yeast

Measuring the dough enhancer.

Tip

Barley malt syrup is available from health food stores. It gives a light, malty flavour to the bread. Use light muscovado sugar if unavailable.

Barley and Oatmeal Bread

Adding oatmeal.

A well-flavoured bread with a dense texture.

Remove the bread pan from the machine. Pour in the milk. Add the butter, barley malt syrup and salt. Add the flours and oatmeal, making sure that the liquid is completely covered. Place the enhancer in one corner. Sprinkle the yeast over the flour. If your machine recommends that you add the dry ingredients first, simply reverse the order that you add them to the pan.

Fit the bread pan in the machine, set the programme to the basic setting, medium crust, and press start.

When the cycle is complete, switch off the machine. Using oven gloves, carefully remove the pan. Turn out the bread onto a wire rack to cool.

Ingredients

275ml/9½fl oz milk
25g/1oz butter
2 tbsp barley malt syrup
1½ tsp salt
250g/9oz strong white
  bread flour
100g/4oz barley flour
50g/2oz fine oatmeal
50g/2oz coarse oatmeal
1 tbsp dough enhancer (see
  page 16)
1½ tsp fast-acting dried yeast

Tip

Barley malt syrup is available from health food stores. It gives a light, malty flavour to the bread. Use light muscovado sugar if unavailable.

Buckwheat Bread

Adding buckwheat flakes.

Buckwheat is, in fact, a seed, which is rich in Vitamin A and B and calcium. Buckwheat flour is grey and has a strong flavour. This is a filling bread that is good for sandwiches.

Remove the bread pan from the machine. Pour in the water. Add the butter, sugar and salt. Add the flour, making sure that the water is completely covered. Place the dough enhancer and milk powder in one corner. Sprinkle the yeast over the flour. If your machine recommends that you add the dry ingredients first, simply reverse the order that you add them to the pan.

Fit the bread pan in the machine, set the programme to the basic setting, medium crust, and press start.

When the cycle is complete, switch off the machine. Using oven gloves, carefully remove the pan. Turn out the bread onto a wire rack to cool.

Ingredients

275ml/9½fl oz water
50g/2oz butter
1 tbsp sugar
1½ tsp salt
250g/9oz strong white bread flour
125g/4½oz buckwheat flour
75g/3oz buckwheat flakes
1 tbsp dough enhancer (see page 16)
1 tbsp milk powder
1 tsp fast-acting dried yeast

Soya Bread

Soya flour adds colour and flavour to this bread. Remove the bread pan from the machine.

Pour in the water. Add the butter, sugar and salt. Add the flours, making sure that the water is completely covered. Place the milk powder in one corner. Sprinkle the yeast over the flour. If your machine recommends that you add the dry ingredients first, simply reverse the order that you add them to the pan.

Fit the bread pan in the machine, set the programme to the basic setting, medium crust, and press start.

When the cycle is complete, switch off the machine. Using oven gloves, carefully remove the pan. Turn out the bread onto a wire rack to cool.

Adding water.

Ingredients

250ml/9fl oz water
25g/1oz butter
1 tbsp sugar
1½ tsp salt
350g/12oz strong white
    bread flour
100g/4oz toasted soya
    flour
2 tbsp dried milk powder
1 tsp fast-acting dried yeast

Adding soya flour.

Rye and Buckwheat Bread

Add the flours.

Sprinkle in the dough enhancer.

Ingredients

275ml/9½fl oz water

2 tbsp olive oil

1 tbsp light muscovado sugar

1½ tsp salt

250g/9oz strong white bread flour

100g/3½oz rye flour

100g/3½oz buckwheat flour

3 tbsp rye flour flakes

2 tbsp dried milk powder

1 tbsp dough enhancer (see page 16)

1½ tsp fast-acting dried yeast

This dense bread is perfect served with strong-flavoured cheeses or for a satisfying sandwich.

Remove the bread pan from the machine. Pour in the water. Add the oil, sugar and salt. Add the flours and rye flakes, making sure that the water is completely covered. Place the milk powder and dough enhancer in one corner. Sprinkle the yeast over the flour. If your machine recommends that you add the dry ingredients first, simply reverse the order that you add them to the pan.

Fit the bread pan in the machine, set the programme to the basic setting, medium crust, and press start.

When the cycle is complete, switch off the machine. Using oven gloves, carefully remove the pan. Turn out the bread onto a wire rack to cool.

Bulgur Wheat

Adding the soaked bulgur wheat.

Ingredients

50g/2oz bulgur wheat
boiling water
225ml/8fl oz water
25g/1oz butter
1 tbsp caster sugar
1½ tsp salt
350g/12oz strong white
   bread flour
100g/4oz strong
   wholemeal bread flour
2 tbsp dried milk powder
1 tsp fast-acting dried yeast

Bulgur wheat gives this bread a moist, nutty texture.

Place the bulgur wheat in a heatproof bowl and cover with plenty of boiling water. Allow to stand for 20 minutes and drain well.

Remove the bread pan from the machine. Place the soaked bulgur wheat in the pan, then pour in the water. Add the butter, sugar and salt. Add the flour, making sure that the water is completely covered.

Bulgur wheat before and after soaking.

Place the milk powder in one corner. Sprinkle the yeast over the flour. If your machine recommends that you add dry ingredients first, reverse the order that you add them to the pan.

Fit the bread pan in the machine, set the programme to the basic setting, medium crust, and press start. During the kneading cycle check the consistency of the dough, adding extra water or a little extra flour if required.

When the cycle is complete, switch off the machine. Using oven gloves, carefully remove the pan. Turn out the bread onto a wire rack to cool.

Tip

The amount of the water the bulgur wheat absorbs may vary and will affect the end result. It is, therefore, important to check the consistency of the dough during kneading; it should have formed a soft but not sticky ball.

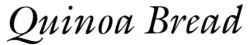

Quinoa Bread

Quinoa was one of the most sacred foods of the ancient Incas of South America. They called it the "mother grain". Quinoa is nutritionally superior to other grains because it is a complete protein, containing all eight essential amino acids.

It is not actually a grain but a seed, and is gluten free. Most quinoa bread recipes use quinoa flour but this can be quite difficult to obtain, even from health food shops. However, whole quinoa is more readily available in health food shops and some larger supermarkets, so I have used it in this recipe.

Place the quinoa in a saucepan and add the boiling water. Cook over a medium heat until the germs separate – about 10 minutes. Remove from the heat. Allow the quinoa to cool and absorb the remaining water.

Remove the bread pan from the machine. Place the cooked quinoa in the pan and then pour in the water. Add the oil, sugar and salt. Add the flours, making sure that the water is completely covered. Sprinkle the yeast over the flour. If your machine recommends that you add the dry ingredients first, simply reverse the order that you add them to the pan.

Fit the bread pan in the machine, set the programme to the basic

Ingredients
50g/2oz quinoa
100ml/4fl oz boiling water
225ml/8fl oz water
2 tbsp sunflower oil
1 tbsp caster sugar
1½ tsp salt
250g/9oz strong white
  bread flour
200g/7oz strong brown
  bread flour
1 tsp fast-acting dried yeast

setting, medium crust, and press start. During the kneading cycle, check the consistency of the dough, which should have formed a smooth, soft, but not sticky ball. Add extra water or a little extra flour if required.

When the cycle is complete, switch off the machine. Using oven gloves, carefully remove the pan. Turn out the bread onto a wire rack to cool.

Adding yeast.

Adding the cooked quinoa.

Light Rye and Caraway

Ingredients
275ml/9½fl oz water
25g/1oz butter
2 tbsp light muscovado
   sugar
1½ tsp salt
200g/7oz rye flour
150g/5oz strong white
   bread flour
100g/4oz strong
   wholemeal bread flour
1 tbsp caraway seeds
1 tsp fast acting dried yeast

Rye bread is often flavoured with caraway as the two flavours go so well together. It has a mild flavour, which is ideal for sandwiches

Remove the bread pan from the machine. Pour in the water. Add the butter, sugar and salt. Add the flours, making sure that the water is completely covered. Place the caraway seeds in one corner. Sprinkle the yeast over the flour. If your machine recommends that you add the dry ingredients first, simply

Weighing the flour.

Adding the rye flour.

reverse the order that you add them to the pan.

Fit the bread pan in the machine, set the programme to the basic setting, medium crust, and press start.

When the cycle is complete, switch off the machine. Using oven gloves, carefully remove the pan. Turn out the bread onto a wire rack to cool.

Rye bread sandwich.

Sun-dried Tomato and Black Olive

Adding olive oil.

Adding olives.

Ingredients

240ml/8½fl oz water
2 tbsp olive oil
1 tbsp sugar
1 tsp salt
300g/10½oz strong white
 bread flour
150g/5oz strong
 wholemeal bread flour
1 tsp fast-acting dried yeast
75g/3oz sun-dried
 tomatoes in oil, drained,
 and chopped
75g/3oz pitted black olives,
 chopped

A fabulous Italian inspired bread, which is great served with antipasto or pasta.

Remove the bread pan from the machine. Pour in the water. Add the oil, sugar and salt. Add the flour, making sure that the water is completely covered. Sprinkle the yeast over the flour. If your machine recommends that you add the dry ingredients first, simply reverse

the order that you add them to the pan.

Fit the bread pan in the machine, set the programme to the basic setting, light crust, and press start. When the machine beeps for extra ingredients, or about 5 minutes before the end of kneading, add the sun-dried tomatoes and olives to the pan.

When the cycle is complete, switch off the machine. Using oven gloves, carefully remove the pan. Turn out the bread onto a wire rack to cool.

Rosemary and Sultana Bread

Ingredients

275ml/9½floz water
3 tbsp olive oil
1 tbsp light muscovado
  sugar
1½ tsp salt
350g/12oz strong white
  bread flour
100g/4oz strong
  wholemeal bread flour
2 tbsp dried milk powder
1 tbsp chopped fresh
  rosemary, or 1 tsp dried
  rosemary
1 tsp fast-acting dried yeast
75g/3oz sultanas

This savoury bread is delicious served with cheese.

Remove the bread pan from the machine. Pour in the water. Add the oil, sugar and salt. Add the flours, making sure that the water is completely covered. Place the milk powder in one corner and the rosemary in another. Sprinkle the yeast over the flour. If your machine

Chopping the rosemary.

recommends that you add the dry ingredients first, simply reverse the order that you add them to the pan.

Fit the bread pan in the machine, set the programme to the basic setting, light crust, and press start When the machine beeps for extra ingredients, or about 5 minutes before the end of kneading, add the sultanas to the pan.

When the cycle is complete, switch off the machine. Using oven gloves, carefully remove the pan. Turn out the bread onto a wire rack to cool.

Add sultanas about 5 minutes before the end of kneading.

Stilton and Walnut

Chopping the walnuts.

Ingredients

240ml/8½fl oz water
2 tbsp walnut oil
1 tbsp caster sugar
½ tsp salt
100g/4oz stilton, crumbled
250g/9oz strong white
  bread flour
200g/7oz strong
  wholemeal bread flour
1 tbsp dried milk powder
  (optional)
1 tsp fast-acting dried yeast
75g/3oz walnuts, chopped

A fabulous savoury bread packed full of flavour. Good for snacking on at any time, or serve with a hearty casserole. Using walnut oil (available from large supermarkets and delis), adds extra depth to the flavour, but you could substitute sunflower oil instead.

Remove the bread pan from the machine. Pour in the water. Add the oil, sugar, salt and cheese. Add the flours, making sure that the water is completely covered. Place the milk powder, if using, in one corner. Sprinkle the yeast over the flour. If your machine recommends that you add the dry ingredients first, simply reverse the order that you add them to the pan.

Fit the bread pan in the machine, set the programme to the basic setting, light crust, and press start. When the machine beeps for extra ingredients, or about 5 minutes before the end of kneading, add the walnuts to the pan.

When the cycle is complete, switch off the machine. Using oven gloves, carefully remove the pan. Turn out the bread onto a wire rack to cool.

Add walnuts about 5 minutes before the end of kneading.

Herb Bread

Ingredients

240ml/8½fl oz water
2 tbsp olive oil
1 tbsp light muscovado
   sugar
1½ tsp salt
2 tbsp chopped fresh parsley
2 tbsp chopped fresh basil
1 tbsp chopped fresh
   rosemary
1 tbsp chopped fresh thyme
450g/1lb strong white
   bread flour
2 tbsp dried milk powder
   (optional)
1 tsp fast-acting dried yeast

Adding herbs to the bread gives the flavour a lift and makes a bread that is ideal with most meals. You can vary the type of herbs used.

Chop the herbs just before using.

If substituting dried herbs, reduce the quantity by two-thirds. The flavour will be different to bread made with fresh herbs but is, nonetheless, very acceptable.

Remove the bread pan from the machine. Pour in the water. Add the oil, sugar, salt and herbs. Add the flour, making sure that the water is completely covered. Place the milk powder, if using, in one corner. Sprinkle the yeast over the flour. If your machine recommends that you add the dry ingredients first, simply reverse the order

that you add them to the pan.

Fit the bread pan in the machine, set the programme to the basic setting, medium crust, and press start.

When the cycle is complete, switch off the machine. Using oven gloves, carefully remove the pan. Turn out the bread onto a wire rack to cool.

Halloumi and Mint Bread

Weighing the flour.

Sprinkle the yeast over the flour. If your machine recommends that you add the dry ingredients first, simply reverse the order that you add them to the pan.

Fit the bread pan in the machine, set the programme to the basic setting, medium crust, and press start.

When the cycle is complete, switch off the machine. Using oven gloves, carefully remove the pan. Turn out the bread onto a wire rack to cool.

Ingredients
240ml/8½fl oz water
4 tbsp olive oil, preferably Greek
1 tbsp caster sugar
1½ tsp salt
150g/5oz halloumi cheese, diced
5 tbsp chopped fresh mint, or 1 tbsp dried mint
450g/1lb strong white bread flour
2 tbsp dried milk powder (optional)
1 tsp fast acting dried yeast

Adding the halloumi cheese.

This is a traditional Cypriot bread. You can use dried mint, but I prefer the flavour of fresh mint.

Remove the bread pan from the machine. Pour in the water. Add the oil, sugar and salt. Add the cheese and mint. Add the flour, making sure that the water is completely covered. Place the milk powder, if using, in one corner.

Savoury Spiced Bread

Adding the spices.

Ingredients
240ml/8½fl oz water
3 tbsp olive oil
1 tbsp sugar
1½ tsp salt
450g/1lb strong white
    bread flour
2 tsp cumin seeds
1 tsp fennel seeds
2 tsp ground coriander
1 tsp ground chilli
1 tsp fast-acting dried yeast

This bread is a really good accompaniment to savoury dishes and adds extra flavour to sandwiches.

Remove the bread pan from the machine. Pour in the water. Add the oil, sugar and salt. Add the flour, making sure that the water is completely covered. Place the whole and ground spices in one corner. Sprinkle the yeast over the flour. If your machine recommends that you add the dry ingredients first, simply reverse the order that you add them to the pan.

Fit the bread pan in the machine, set the programme to the basic setting, medium crust, and press start.

When the cycle is complete, switch off the machine. Using oven gloves, carefully remove the pan. Turn out the bread onto a wire rack to cool.

Adding the oil.

Potato and Caraway Bread

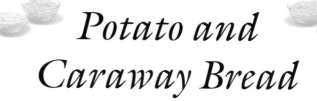

Adding the salt.

Cook potato until just tender.

Ingredients
300ml/10 fl oz water
225g/8oz potato, peeled
and diced
25g/1oz butter
1 tbsp sugar
1½ tsp salt
450g/1lb strong white
bread flour
2 tbsp milk powder
1 tbsp caraway seeds
1 tsp fast-acting dried yeast

To complete (optional):
1 tsp cornflour
1 tbsp water
pinch salt
caraway seeds to sprinkle

Place the water in a saucepan and bring to the boil. Add the potato and simmer for 5 to 8 minutes until the potatoes are just tender. Drain, reserving 200ml/7fl oz of the cooking liquid.

Return the potatoes to the heat for a few seconds to get rid of any excess moisture. Mash and allow to cool.

Remove the bread pan from the machine. Pour in the reserved cooking liquid. Add the butter, sugar and salt. Add the flour, making sure that the water is completely covered. Add the mashed potato and place the milk powder and caraway seeds in one corner. Sprinkle the yeast over the flour. If your machine recommends that you add the dry ingredients first, simply reverse the order that you add them to the pan.

Fit the bread pan in the machine, set the programme to the basic setting, medium crust, and press start.

If desired, just before the baking cycle starts, mix the cornflour, water and salt together, open the lid, brush the top of the risen dough with the

Tip
If using leftover mash with added milk and butter, reduce the amount of liquid added to the dough. Check dough consistency during kneading.

cornflour mixture and sprinkle with a few extra caraway seeds. Quickly close the lid.

When the cycle is complete, switch off the machine. Using oven gloves, carefully remove the pan. Turn out the bread onto a wire rack to cool.

Carrot and Cumin

Adding the flour

When the cycle is complete, switch off the machine. Using oven gloves, carefully remove the pan. Turn out the bread onto a wire rack to cool.

Ingredients
240ml/8½fl oz water
175g/6oz carrot, grated
25g/1oz butter
1 tbsp light muscovado
    sugar
1 tsp salt
450g/1lb strong white
    bread flour
1 tbsp ground cumin
1 tbsp cumin seeds
1 tsp fast acting dried yeast

A savoury bread with a moist crumb and a slightly sweet flavour. Try serving it with soup.

Remove the bread pan from the machine. Pour in the water. Add the carrot, butter, sugar and salt. Add the flour, making sure that the water is completely covered. Add the ground cumin and seeds. Sprinkle the yeast over the flour. If your machine recommends that you add the dry ingredients first, simply reverse the order that you add them to the pan.

Fit the bread pan in the machine, set the programme to the basic setting, medium crust, and press start.

Grating carrot.

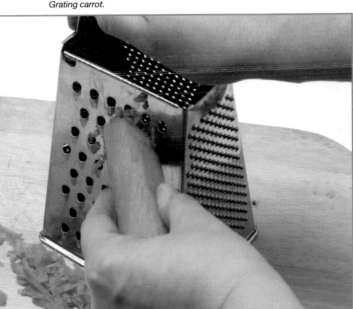

Soda Bread

Slashing the bread.

Soda bread is not mixed in the machine because it does not need the long mixing and kneading times.

Mix the flour, bicarbonate of soda and salt together in a mixing bowl. Rub in the butter with your fingertips until well combined. Add the buttermilk to the bowl and mix to form a smooth dough. Knead for about 1 minute.

Take the pan out of the machine and remove the paddle. Shape the soda bread to fit the machine and place in the pan. Carefully cut a deep slash in the top of the dough, taking care not to scratch the tin.

Fit the bread pan in the machine, set the programme to the bake-only setting and press start.

Check the bread after 1 hour 15 minutes; it should be golden brown and well risen.

When the bread is cooked, switch off the machine. Using oven gloves, carefully remove the pan. Turn out the bread onto a wire rack to cool.

Ingredients

400g/14oz plain white flour

2 tsp bicarbonate of soda

¼ tsp salt

50g/2oz butter, cut into small cubes

284ml carton buttermilk

Adding the buttermilk.

Chilli Corn Bread

Add the wet ingredients to the dry ingredients.

Ingredients

225g/8oz fine cornmeal
100g/4oz plain flour
1 tsp dried chilli flakes
2 tsp baking powder
½ tsp bicarbonate of soda
½ tsp salt
2 large eggs
150ml/¼pt milk
150g/5oz carton natural
  yogurt
1 sweet pointed pepper,
  seeded and chopped
6 tbsp sweetcorn niblets
1 red chilli, seeded and
  chopped
25g/1oz butter, melted

Serve with salads, stews, grilled meats and barbecued food or just buttered.

Place the cornmeal, flour, chilli flakes, baking powder, soda and salt in a large mixing bowl and stir well to combine.

Place the eggs, milk and yogurt in another bowl and whisk until well combined.

Make a well in the centre of the dry ingredients and pour in the yogurt mixture. Add the pepper, sweetcorn, chilli and melted butter and mix with a wooden spoon, until just blended.

Remove the bread pan from the machine, spoon the cornbread mixture into pan and level the top.

Fit the bread pan in the machine, set the programme to the bake-only setting for 50 minutes and press start.

Check the bread is cooked – a skewer inserted into the centre should come out clean. Increase baking time if required.

When the bread is cooked, switch off the machine. Using oven gloves, carefully remove the pan. Turn out the bread onto a wire rack to cool.

Red chilli.

Cinnamon Nut and Raisin Bread

A slightly sweet bread that is delicious eaten plain or spread with cream cheese and topped with jam or fruit.

Remove the bread pan from the machine. Pour in the water. Add the butter, sugar and salt. Add the flour, making sure that the water is covered completely. Place the cinnamon in one corner. Sprinkle the yeast over the flour. If your machine recommends that you add the dry ingredients first, simply reverse the order that you add them to the pan.

Adding sugar.

Ingredients
250ml/9fl oz water
75g/3oz butter
3 tbsp light muscovado sugar
1 tsp salt
450g/1lb strong white bread flour
2 tsp ground cinnamon
1 tsp fast-acting dried yeast
50g/2oz chopped almonds, hazelnuts or pecan nuts
50g/2oz raisins

Fit the bread pan in the machine, set the programme to the basic setting, light crust, and press start. When the machine beeps for extra ingredients, or about 5 minutes before the end of kneading, add the raisins and almonds to the pan.

When the cycle is complete, switch off the machine. Using oven gloves, carefully remove the pan. Turn out the bread onto a wire rack to cool.

Adding raisins before the end of kneading.

Honey Buttermilk Bread

Adding buttermilk.

Adding honey.

Ingredients

284ml carton buttermilk
50ml/2fl oz water
3 tbsp honey
1 tsp salt
500g/1lb 2oz strong white
   bread flour
1½ tsp fast acting dried yeast

To complete:

honey

A sweet bread not dissimilar in texture to the French brioche. It is delicious toasted and spread with jam. It has very good keeping qualities and will last for 3 to 4 days if kept wrapped – that is if it hasn't disappeared long before that!

Remove the bread pan from the machine. Pour in the buttermilk and water. Add the honey and salt. Add the flour, making sure that the liquid is completely covered. Sprinkle the yeast over the flour. If your machine recommends that you add the dry ingredients first, simply reverse the order that you add them to the pan.

Fit the bread pan in the machine, set the programme to the basic setting, medium crust, and press start.

When the cycle is complete, switch off the machine. Using oven gloves, carefully remove the pan. Turn out the bread onto a wire rack to cool.

While the bread is still hot brush the top with honey.

Honey and Walnut Loaf

Chopping walnuts.

Ingredients

240ml/8½fl oz water

5 tbsp clear honey

2 tbsp walnut oil

1½ tsp salt

450g/1lb strong white
bread flour

2 tbsp milk powder

1 tsp fast-acting dried yeast

100g/4oz walnuts,
chopped

To complete:

honey

The type of honey you use will affect the flavour of the bread. Experiment with different honey to find your favourite. Orange blossom honey is mine.

Remove the bread pan from the machine. Pour in the water. Add the honey, walnut oil and salt. Add the flour, making sure that the water is completely covered. Place the milk powder in one corner. Sprinkle the yeast over the flour. If your machine recommends that you add the dry ingredients first, simply reverse the order that you add them to the pan.

Fit the bread pan in the machine, set the programme to the basic setting, light crust, and press start. When the machine beeps for extra ingredients, or about 5 minutes before the end of kneading, add the walnuts to the pan.

When the cycle is complete, switch off the machine. Using oven gloves, carefully remove the pan. Turn out the bread onto a wire rack to cool.

While the bread is still hot brush the top with honey.

Adding walnuts.

Vanilla Cherry Bread

Adding flour.

Add cherries 5 minutes before the end of kneading.

Ingredients
225ml/8fl oz milk
1 tsp vanilla essence
50g/2oz butter
3 tbsp sugar
1 tsp salt
450g/1lb strong white
 bread flour
1 tsp fast-acting dried yeast
100g/4oz glacé cherries,
 halved

To complete:
2 tbsp icing sugar
¼ tsp vanilla essence
1 tbsp cold water

A sweet bread best served spread with cherry jam or lightly toasted.

Remove the bread pan from the machine. Pour in the milk. Add the vanilla essence, butter, sugar and salt. Add the flour, making sure that the milk is completely covered. Sprinkle the yeast over the flour. If your machine recommends that you add the dry ingredients first, simply reverse the order that you add them to the pan.

Fit the bread pan in the machine, set the programme to the basic setting, light crust, and press start. When the machine beeps for extra ingredients, or about 5 minutes before the end of kneading, add the cherries to the pan.

When the cycle is complete, switch off the machine. Using oven gloves, carefully remove the pan. Turn out the bread onto a wire rack to cool.

While the bread is still hot, combine the icing sugar, vanilla essence and cold water, and brush over the top of the bread.

Brioche Loaf

Adding the eggs to the pan.

Ingredients

75ml/3fl oz milk
3 eggs
50g/2oz butter
3 tbsp caster sugar
½ tsp salt
450g/1lb strong white
  bread flour
2 tbsp dried milk powder
1 tsp fast-acting dried yeast
100g/4oz sultanas or
  raisins (optional)

To complete:
beaten egg to glaze

In France this classic sweet bread is often made as small individual buns and served with coffee. However, it also makes the most wonderful sweet toast, and is delicious served with jam or lemon curd. Use to make bread and butter pudding for a divine dessert.

Remove the bread pan from the machine. Pour in the milk. Add the eggs, butter, sugar and salt. Add the flour, making sure that the water is completely covered. Place the milk powder in one corner. Sprinkle the yeast over the flour. If your machine recommends that you add the dry ingredients first, simply reverse the order that you add them to the pan.

Fit the bread pan in the machine, set the programme to the basic setting, light crust, and press start. If using, add dried fruit to the pan when the machine beeps for extra ingredients, or about 5 minutes before the end of kneading.

Working quickly, just before the baking cycle starts, open the lid and brush the top of the loaf with beaten egg. Close the lid.

When the cycle is complete, switch off the machine. Using oven gloves, carefully remove the pan. Turn out the bread onto a wire rack to cool.

Add sultanas or raisins for a fruity version of this loaf.

Bun Loaf

Adding sugar.

Add the dried fruits towards the end of the kneading cycle..

A sweet fruit loaf that is delicious served fresh or toasted with plenty of butter.

Remove the bread pan from the machine. Pour in the water. Add the butter, sugar and salt. Add the flour, making sure that the water is completely covered. Place the milk powder in one corner. Sprinkle the yeast over the flour. If your machine recommends that you add the dry ingredients first, simply reverse the order that you add them to the pan.

Fit the bread pan in the machine, set the programme to the basic setting, light crust, and press start. When the machine beeps for extra ingredients, or about 5 minutes before the end of kneading, add the mixed dried fruit to the pan.

When the cycle is complete, switch off the machine. Using oven gloves, carefully remove the pan. Turn out the bread onto a wire rack to cool.

Ingredients

240ml/8½fl oz water
25g/1oz butter
4 tbsp light muscovado
  sugar
1 tsp salt
450g/1lb strong white
  bread flour
2 tbsp dried milk powder
1 tsp fast-acting dried yeast
150g/5oz luxury mixed
  dried fruit

Sugar glaze:

1 tbsp caster sugar
1 tbsp water

To make the sugar glaze, place the sugar and water in a small pan and heat. Stir until the sugar dissolves. Brush over the hot loaf to glaze.

Tip

Regular dried mixed fruit can be used but this loaf is particularly good made with a luxury mix, which contains other dried fruits such as apricots, pineapple, chopped peel and cherries.

Apple and Pomegranate Loaf

Peel, core and grate the apples.

Ingredients
200ml/7fl oz water
50g/2oz butter
1 tsp lemon juice
1 green eating apple,
 peeled, cored and grated
4 tbsp light muscovado
 sugar
1 tsp salt
1 pomegranate
450g/1lb strong white
 bread flour
2 tbsp dried milk powder
1½ tsp fast-acting dried yeast

This sweet bread has a delicious crunch from the pomegranate seeds

Remove the bread pan from the machine. Pour in the water. Add the butter, lemon juice, apple, sugar and salt. Cut the pomegranate in half and scoop out the flesh and seeds, discarding the white pith. Add to the pan. Add the flour, making sure that the water and fruit is completely covered. Place the milk powder in one corner. Sprinkle the yeast over the flour. If your machine recommends that you add the dry ingredients first, simply reverse the order that you add them to the pan.

Fit the bread pan in the machine, set the programme to the basic setting, medium crust, and press start.

When the cycle is complete, switch off the machine. Using oven gloves, carefully remove the pan. Turn out the bread onto a wire rack to cool.

Scoop out the pomegranate seeds.

Saffron Bread

A slightly sweet bread with a fabulous subtle flavour, saffron bread is best served plain with butter so that its flavour is not masked.

Heat the milk in a small saucepan until almost boiling. Add the saffron, stir and remove from the heat. Allow to stand for 20 minutes.

Remove the bread pan from the machine. Pour in the milk. Add the egg, butter, sugar and salt. Add the flour, making sure that the liquid is completely covered. Sprinkle the yeast over the flour. If your machine recommends that you add the dry ingredients first, simply reverse the order that you add them to the pan.

Fit the bread pan in the machine, set the programme to the basic setting, medium crust, and press start.

When the cycle is complete, switch off the machine. Using oven gloves, carefully remove the pan. Turn out the bread onto a wire rack to cool.

Adding the milk.

Ingredients
200ml/7fl oz milk
1 tsp saffron threads
1 egg
50g/2oz butter
50g/2oz icing sugar
½ tsp salt
450g/1lb strong white
   bread flour
1 tsp fast-acting dried yeast

Add saffron to the hot milk and allow it to infuse..

Date and Walnut

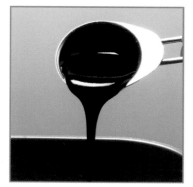

Adding date syrup.

Add walnuts towards the end of kneading.

Ingredients

240ml/8½fl oz water
2 tbsp walnut oil
2 tbsp date syrup, or 2 tbsp
   light moscovado sugar
1½ tsp salt
450g/1lb strong white
   bread flour
2 tbsp dried milk powder
1 tsp fast-acting dried yeast
75g/3oz pitted dates,
   chopped
75g/3oz walnuts, chopped

To complete:

2 tbsp icing sugar
1 tbsp water

The combination of walnuts and dates is a classic that works well in both cakes and breads. You could try using pecans instead of the walnuts or figs instead of the dates.

Remove the bread pan from the machine. Pour in the water. Add the oil, syrup or sugar and salt. Add the flour, making sure that the water is completely covered. Place the milk powder in one corner. Sprinkle the yeast over the flour. If your machine recommends that you add the dry ingredients first, simply reverse the order that you add them to the pan.

Fit the bread pan in the machine, set the programme to the basic setting, light crust, and press start. When the machine beeps for extra ingredients, or about 5 minutes

before the end of kneading, add the dates and walnuts.

When the cycle is complete, switch off the machine. Using oven gloves, carefully remove the pan. Turn out the bread onto a wire rack to cool.

Mix the icing sugar and water together and brush over the bread while it is still hot.

Tip

Walnut oil is available from large supermarkets. Once open it will last three months if stored in a cool dark place. It is fabulous used in salad dressings. Date syrup is available from health food stores. It makes a delicious sauce served on ice cream. You can also use it as a sweetener in baking or on breakfast cereals.

Chocolate Chip and Peanut Bread

Adding the peanut butter.

Ingredients

240ml/8½fl oz water
150g/5oz peanut butter
1 tbsp sugar
½ tsp salt
450g/1lb strong white
  bread flour
1 tsp fast-acting dried yeast
100g/4oz plain chocolate
  chips

A sweet bread that is delicious served on its own or spread with a little chocolate spread or extra peanut butter.

Remove the bread pan from the machine. Pour in the water. Add the peanut butter, sugar and salt. Add the flour, making sure that the water is completely covered. Sprinkle the yeast over the flour. If your machine recommends that you add the dry ingredients first, simply reverse the order that you add them to the pan.

Fit the bread pan in the machine, set the programme to the basic setting, light crust, and press start. When the machine beeps for extra ingredients, or about 5 minutes before the end of kneading, add the chocolate chips to the pan.

When the cycle is complete, switch off the machine. Using oven gloves, carefully remove the pan. Turn out the bread onto a wire rack to cool.

Add chocolate chips towards the end of kneading.

SHAPE
AND
BAKE

Once you have mastered the basic breads, or when you have a little more time on your hands, you may wish to take your bread making one step further, and finish the bread yourself. This opens up a much wider variety of shapes and fillings.

All the recipes for breads baked in the pan can also be made on the dough setting, shaped, and left for the final rise before baking in a conventional oven. Some of the breads in this section can also be made and baked in the machine on the basic setting for a standard loaf. These are indicated on the recipe.

Set the programme to the dough setting. This will knead the bread and keep the dough at the correct temperature for the first rising. When the dough cycle is complete, turn out the dough and knock back. (This is the term used for the simple step of knocking the air out of the risen dough.) The dough should then be lightly kneaded and shaped as desired.

Leave the dough to prove (the name given to the second rising). It should be left loosely covered in a warm place until almost doubled in size. Do not let the dough rise too much or it may collapse.

The dough must be covered or the surface will dry out and stop the dough from expanding properly. Do not cover it too tightly as this will also inhibit the dough from rising. You can cover the dough with lightly oiled cling wrap. A clean, damp tea towel or a tea towel that has been dusted with flour can also be used. I find that slipping the tin or tray into a clean carrier bag is a very convenient way of covering the dough, as well as making use of the many bags that seem to clutter up my kitchen drawer.

A warm place will enable the dough to expand at the quickest rate but very often dough that rises more slowly has a better texture. If you can spare the time, let the dough rise in a cool room. Dough can even be allowed to rise very slowly, e.g. overnight in the refrigerator.

To complete, glaze the dough if required and bake in a hot oven. To test if the bread is cooked, tap the bottom of the loaf with your knuckles – the loaf should sound hollow.

Dark Rye

Shape the dough into an oval.

Sprinkle with rye flakes.

Ingredients

200ml/7fl oz water
1 tbsp sunflower oil
2 tbsp black treacle
1 tsp salt
175g/6oz rye flour
175g/6oz strong white
   bread flour
2 tbsp milk powder
1 tbsp cocoa powder
1½ tsp fast-acting dried yeast

To complete:
beaten egg to glaze
rye flakes

The cocoa and treacle give the dark colour to this rye bread and add an interesting depth to the flavour.

Remove the bread pan from the machine. Pour in the water. Add the oil, treacle and salt. Add the flours, making sure that the water is completely covered. Place the milk powder and cocoa powder in one corner. Sprinkle the yeast over the flour. If your machine recommends that you add the dry ingredients first, simply reverse the order that you add them to the pan.

Fit the bread pan in the machine, set the programme to the dough setting and press start. When the cycle has finished, transfer the dough to a lightly floured work surface. Knock back and lightly knead.

Shape the loaf into an oval and place on a lightly oiled baking sheet. Cover loosely and allow to rise in a warm place. Because of the rye content the loaf will not rise as much as a white loaf.

Preheat the oven to 200°C/400°F/ gas mark 6. Brush the top of the loaf with beaten egg and sprinkle some rye flakes on top. Bake for about 30 minutes or until the loaf sounds hollow when tapped underneath.

Variation:

You can use wholemeal or brown flour in place of the white bread flour. This will produce a loaf with a denser texture.

Tip

The dough can also be made and baked on a basic programme to make a simple loaf.

Fig and Thyme Bread

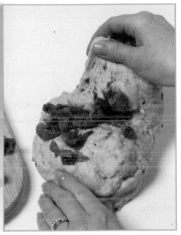

Knead in the chopped figs.

A savoury bread that has fabulous flavour and is great with antipasto.

Remove the bread pan from the machine. Pour in the water. Add the olive oil, sugar and salt. Add the flours, making sure that the water is completely covered. Place the thyme in one corner. Sprinkle the yeast over the flour. If your machine recommends that you add the dry ingredients first, simply reverse the order that you add them to the pan.

Fit the bread pan in the machine, set the programme to the dough setting and press start.

When the dough cycle has finished, transfer the dough to a lightly floured work surface. Knock back and lightly knead. Knead in the chopped figs. Shape the dough into an elongated loaf and place on a lightly greased baking sheet.

Cover with oiled cling wrap and leave in a warm place to rise until doubled in size. Take a sharp knife and slash the bread along its length. Sprinkle with flour. Bake in a preheated oven 220°C/425°F/gas mark 7 for about 30 to 35 minutes, or until golden and the loaf sounds hollow when tapped underneath.

Transfer to a wire rack to cool.

Ingredients

240ml/8½fl oz water
2 tbsp olive oil
1 tbsp dark muscovado sugar
1½ tsp salt
250g/9oz strong white bread flour
200g/7oz granary flour
1 tbsp fresh thyme leaves
1 tsp fast-acting dried yeast
100g/4oz dried figs
flour to sprinkle

Tip

The dough can also be made and baked on basic programme to make a simple loaf. Add the figs when the machine bleeps for extra ingredients, or 5 minutes before the end of kneading.

Focaccia with Sun-dried Tomato and Oregano

Adding the sun-dried tomatoes.

Remove the bread pan from the machine. Pour in the water and oil. Add the salt and flour, making sure the water is completely covered. Sprinkle the yeast over the flour. If your machine recommends you add the dry ingredients first, reverse the order you add them to the pan.

Fit the bread pan in the machine, set the programme to the dough setting and press start. When the machine beeps for extra ingredients, or about 5 minutes before the end of kneading, add the sun-dried tomatoes to the pan.

When the cycle has finished, transfer the dough to a lightly floured surface. Knock back and lightly knead. Flatten dough into a rough oval about 1cm/½inch thick. Place on a lightly oiled baking sheet. If preferred, divide the dough into two and make two smaller loaves.

Press your fingertips into the dough to make a dimpled effect. Sprinkle oregano and sea salt over the bread. Cover loosely and allow to rise again for 45 minutes to 1 hour.

Preheat the oven to 190°C/375°F/ gas mark 5. Drizzle a little oil over the bread and bake for 20 to 25 minutes, or until golden and the loaf sounds hollow when tapped on the bottom. Cool on a wire rack.

Ingredients

240ml/8½fl oz water
3 tbsp extra virgin olive oil
½ tsp salt
500g/12oz strong white bread flour
1 tsp fast-acting dried yeast
50g/2oz sun-dried tomatoes in oil, chopped

To complete:
dried oregano to sprinkle
sea salt to sprinkle
olive oil to drizzle

Tip

The salt in the bread has been reduced because of the saltiness of the sun-dried tomatoes and the extra salt sprinkled on top. You can use the oil from the jar of tomatoes in place of the olive oil in the bread, but make sure you leave enough in the jar to cover the tomatoes.

Sage and Onion Spiral Loaf

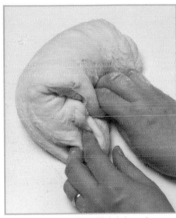

Knock back and lightly knead the dough.

Place the loaf seam-side down in the prepared tin.

Ingredients

240ml/8½fl oz water
2 tbsp olive oil
1 tbsp sugar
1½ tsp salt
450g/1lb strong white
 bread flour
1 tsp fast-acting dried yeast

To complete:

2 tbsp olive oil
1 small onion, finely
 chopped
4 tbsp chopped fresh sage
beaten egg to glaze

Remove the bread pan from the machine. Pour in the water. Add the oil, sugar and salt. Add the flour, making sure that the water is completely covered. Sprinkle the yeast over the flour. If your machine recommends that you add the dry ingredients first, simply reverse the order that you add them to the pan.

Fit the bread pan in the machine, set the programme to the dough setting and press start.

Heat the olive oil in a small frying pan and fry the onion until it is just beginning to soften. Remove from the heat and stir in the sage.

When the dough cycle has finished, transfer the dough to a lightly floured work surface. Knock back and lightly knead. Roll out to form a rectangle about 35 x 23cm/14 x 9in. Brush with beaten egg and spread the sage mixture over the surface. Roll up from the short end. Place the loaf seam-side down in a greased 23 x 13cm/ 9 x 5in loaf tin. Cover loosely and leave in a warm place until doubled in size. Carefully brush the top with beaten egg and bake in a preheated oven 190°C/375°F/gas mark 5 for 45 to 50 minutes, or until golden and the loaf sounds hollow when tapped underneath. Transfer to a wire rack to cool.

Cheesy Garlic Roll

Knock back and lightly knead the dough.

A fabulous savoury loaf that is delicious served with salads as part of a buffet table.

Remove the bread pan from the machine. Pour in the water. Add the oil, sugar and salt. Add the flour, ensuring the water is completely covered. Place the milk powder in one corner and sprinkle the yeast over the flour. If your machine recommends you add the dry ingredients first, reverse the order you add them to the pan.

Fit the bread pan in the machine, set the programme to the dough setting and press start.

Combine the spring onions, garlic, parsley and cottage cheese.

When the dough cycle has finished, transfer the dough to a lightly floured surface. Knock back and lightly knead. Roll out to form a rectangle about 35 x 23cm/14 x 9in. Spread the cheese mixture over the surface, leaving a 2.5cm/1in border along one long edge and a bigger border along one of the short ends.

Ingredients

240ml/8½fl oz water
2 tbsp olive oil
1 tbsp sugar
1½ tsp salt
250g/9oz strong white
  bread flour
200g/7oz wholemeal flour
2 tbsp milk powder
1 tsp fast-acting dried yeast

To complete:

8 spring onions, sliced
2 cloves garlic, chopped
4 tbsp chopped fresh parsley
200g/7oz cottage cheese
15g/½oz butter, melted

Roll up like a swiss roll.

Roll up like a Swiss roll, starting from the other short end. Pinch the ends together to seal in the filling. Place loaf seam-side down on a greased baking sheet. Cover loosely with oiled cling wrap and leave in a warm place until doubled in size. Bake in a preheated oven 190°C/ 375°F/gas mark 5 for about 40 to 45 minutes, or until golden and the loaf sounds hollow when tapped underneath. Brush top with melted butter and cool on a wire rack.

Chive and Parsley Bread Ring

Remove the bread pan from the machine. Pour in the water. Add the butter, sugar and salt. Add the flour, making sure that the water is completely covered. Place the milk powder in one corner and sprinkle the yeast over the flour. If your machine recommends that you add the dry ingredients first, simply reverse the order that you add them to the pan.

Fit the bread pan in the machine, set the programme to the dough setting and press start.

Heat the olive oil in a small frying pan and fry the onion until it is just

Ingredients
240ml/8½fl oz water
25g/1oz butter
1 tbsp sugar
1¼ tsp salt
450g/1lb strong white
   bread flour
2 tbsp milk powder
1 tsp fast-acting dried yeast

To complete:
2 tbsp olive oil
½ small onion, finely
   chopped
1 clove garlic, crushed
   (optional)
3 tbsp snipped fresh chives
2 tbsp chopped fresh parsley

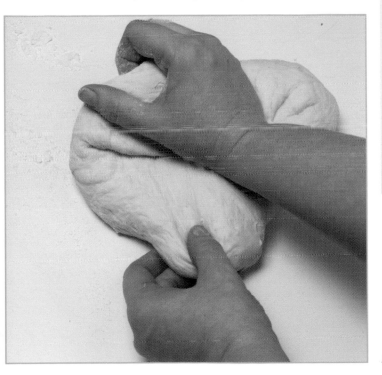

Knock back and lightly knead the dough.

Roll up like a Swiss roll from the long side.

beginning to soften. Stir in the garlic, if using, and cook for a few seconds more. Remove from the heat and stir in the chives and parsley.

When dough cycle has finished, transfer the dough to a lightly floured work surface. Knock back and lightly knead. Roll out to form a rectangle about 30 x 23cm/12 x 9in

Spread the chive and onion mixture over the dough and roll up

Cut into eight equal pieces.

Arrange slicess in the prepared tin.

from the long side like a Swiss roll. Cut into eight equal pieces.

Lightly grease a 23cm/9in loose-bottomed cake tin and arrange the slices equally spaced in the tin. Cover loosely and leave in a warm place to rise for about 45 minutes to 1 hour.

Preheat the oven to 220°C/425°F/gas mark 7. Bake in the centre of the oven for about 35 to 40 minutes until risen and golden. Allow to cool in the tin for a few minutes and then transfer to a wire rack to cool.

Sesame Seed Knots

Toasting the seeds of these flavoursome, attractive, dinner rolls brings out their flavour.

Remove the bread pan from the machine. Pour in the water. Add the oil, sugar and salt. Add the flours, making sure that the water is completely covered. Add the toasted sesame seeds. Place the milk powder in one corner and sprinkle the yeast over the flour. If your machine recommends that you add the dry ingredients first, simply reverse the order that you add them to the pan.

Fit the bread pan in the machine, set the programme to the dough setting.

When the cycle has finished, transfer the dough to a lightly floured work surface. Knock back and lightly knead.

Divide into 10 equal pieces. Roll each piece into a rope about 25cm/10in long. Tie a single knot in each piece and place on a lightly greased baking tray, so that the roll sits on one end of the rope and the other end shows on top. Repeat with the remaining dough and space the pieces on the baking sheet to allow the rolls to expand.

Ingredients

300ml/10fl oz water
2 tbsp sesame seed oil
1 tbsp sugar
1½ tsp salt
200g/7oz wholemeal flour
250g/9oz strong white
  bread flour
75g/3oz toasted sesame
  seeds
2 tbsp milk powder
1¼ tsp fast-acting dried yeast

To complete:

beaten egg or milk to glaze
sesame seeds to sprinkle

kneading the dough.

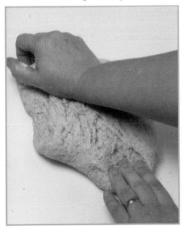

Divide the dough into ten equal pieces.

123

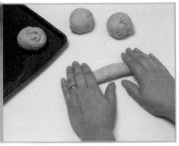

Roll the dough to form a rope

Tie a single knot.

Place the roll on the baking tray so that it sits on the end of the rope.

Cover loosely and leave in a warm place until doubled in volume – for about 45 minutes to 1 hour.

Preheat the oven to 220°C/425°F/ gas mark 7. Lightly brush the tops of the rolls with the beaten egg or milk and sprinkle with sesame seeds. Bake for 12 to 15 minutes, or until the rolls are crisp, golden and sound hollow when tapped underneath.

Tip

Sesame seed oil is available from large supermarkets and oriental stores. It is used extensively to flavour Chinese and Japanese foods. The dough can also be made and baked on basic programme to make a simple loaf.

Sprinkle with sesame sseeds.

Parmesan Batch Rolls

These cheese rolls are delicious served warm with a bowl of steaming soup.

Reserve a little of the parmesan and black pepper to decorate the tops of the rolls.

Remove the bread pan from the machine. Pour in the water. Add the oil, sugar and salt. Add the flours, making sure that the water is completely covered. Place the milk powder, parmesan cheese and crushed peppercorns in one corner and sprinkle the yeast over the flour. If your machine recommends that you add the dry ingredients first, simply reverse the order that you add them to the pan.

Fit the bread pan in the machine, set the programme to the dough setting and press start.

When the dough cycle has finished, transfer the dough to a lightly floured work surface. Knock back and lightly knead.

Divide the dough into 12 equal pieces and roll into balls. Equally space the balls in a lightly greased 25 x 20cm/10 x 8in shallow cake tin or a small roasting tin. Cover loosely and allow to rise in a warm place until doubled in size.

Ingredients

75g/3oz parmesan cheese, grated
1 tbsp black peppercorns, crushed
240ml/8½fl oz water
4 tbsp olive oil
1 tbsp sugar
1½ tsp salt
350g/12oz strong white bread flour
100g/4oz wholemeal flour
2 tbsp milk powder
1 tsp fast-acting dried yeast

To complete:

1 egg yolk mixed with 1 tbsp milk or water

Tip

The dough can also be made and baked on basic programme to make a simple loaf.

Shape the dough into balls.

Sprinkle with cheese and black pepper.

Brush the egg mixture over the dough and sprinkle alternate rolls with the reserved parmesan and black pepper. Bake in a preheated oven at 180°C/350°F/gas mark 4 for 20 minutes until golden. Turn out onto a wire rack to cool.

Seedy Breadsticks

Roll the dough into a long stick.

Brush with beaten egg and sprinkle with seeds.

Ingredients

120ml/4½fl oz water
1 tbsp olive oil
1 tsp sugar
½ tsp salt
150g/5oz strong white
   bread flour
100g/4oz strong brown
   bread flour
½ tsp fast-acting dried yeast

To complete:

beaten egg to glaze
sesame seeds
poppy seeds
sea salt

Serve these Italian-style breadsticks as a pre-dinner nibble with drinks or with dips such as hummus or soured cream and chives.

Remove the bread pan from the machine. Pour in the water. Add the oil, sugar and salt. Add the flours, making sure that the water is completely covered. Sprinkle the yeast over the flour. If your machine recommends that you add the dry ingredients first, simply reverse the order that you add them to the pan.

Fit the bread pan in the machine, set the programme to the dough setting and press start.

When the dough cycle has finished, preheat oven to 200°C/400°F/gas mark 6. Transfer the dough to a lightly floured work surface. Knock back and lightly knead. Break off pieces of the dough about the size of a walnut – and roll each into a long stick about the thickness of a pencil. Place, slightly spaced, on a greased baking sheet.

Brush the sticks of bread with the beaten egg and sprinkle sesame or poppy seeds onto them. Finally give each a light sprinkling of salt. Do not leave the dough to rise after shaping.

Bake for about 10 to 15 minutes until golden and crisp. The sticks should snap easily and not be doughy in the middle. Transfer to a wire rack and cool.

Store in an airtight tin.

Naan with Chilli and Coriander

Indian breads are best served warm. You can reheat them, wrapped in foil in a hot oven for 5 minutes.

Remove the bread pan from the machine. Pour in the water. Add the

Divide each dough piece into a tear-drop shape..

oil, sugar, yogurt and salt. Add the flour, making sure that the liquid is completely covered. Sprinkle the yeast over the flour. If your machine recommends that you add the dry ingredients first, simply reverse the order that you add them to the pan.

Fit the bread pan in the machine, set the programme to the dough setting and press start. When the machine beeps for extra ingredients, or about 5 minutes before the end of kneading, add the chopped coriander, garlic and chilli.

When the cycle has finished, transfer the dough to a lightly floured work surface. Knock back and lightly knead.

Ingredients
175ml/6fl oz water
2 tbsp sunflower oil
1 tsp caster sugar
4 tbsp natural yogurt
1 tsp salt
450g/1lb strong white
  bread flour
1 tsp fast-acting dried yeast

To complete:
6 tbsp chopped fresh
  coriander
2 cloves garlic, crushed
1 red chilli, seeded and
  chopped

Cook in a heavy-based frying pan.

Divide into 6 to 8 equal-size pieces. Using a lightly floured rolling pin, shape each piece into a teardrop shape about 5mm/¼in thick. Place on a lightly greased baking sheet and cover loosely. Leave to rise for about 30 minutes until puffy and doubled in thickness. Heat a heavy-based frying pan over a medium heat and cook in batches for 2 to 3 minutes each side until golden.

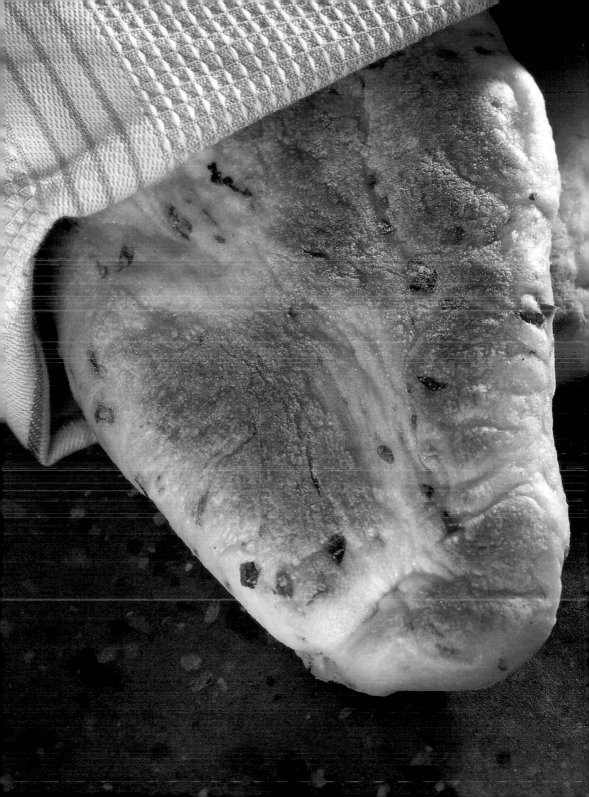

Three-grain Clover Rolls

Adding brown flour.

Place three small balls of dough in each muffin cup.

Ingredients

240ml/8½fl oz water

2 tbsp olive oil

2 tbsp light muscovado
  sugar

1 tsp salt

150g/5oz cooked long
  grain white rice

250g/9oz granary flour

100g/4oz strong brown
  bread flour

100g/4oz strong white
  bread flour

50g/2oz rolled oats

1½ tsp fast-acting dried yeast

To complete:

beaten egg to glaze

sesame, poppy or sunflower
  seeds

These rolls have a surprisingly light texture and look very pretty at the dinner table. If you do not have a muffin tray, simply place the three balls of dough close together on a baking sheet. Why not try making other breads in this attractive shape.

Remove the bread pan from the machine. Pour in the water. Add the oil, sugar, salt and rice. Add the flours, making sure that the water is completely covered. Add the oats. Sprinkle over the yeast. If your machine recommends that you add the dry ingredients first, simply reverse the order that you add them to the pan.

Fit the bread pan in the machine, set the programme to wholemeal dough setting and press start.

Lightly grease a 12-cup muffin tray. When the cycle has finished, transfer the dough to a lightly floured work surface. Knock back and lightly knead. Divide the dough into 12 equal pieces. Divide each piece into three and roll into small balls. Place three balls in each muffin cup. Cover loosely and allow to rise in a warm place until doubled in size.

Gently brush with beaten egg and sprinkle the tops with a few seeds of your choice. Bake in a preheated oven at 200°C/400°F/gas mark 6 for 15 to 20 minutes.

Tip

This is an ideal recipe for using up cooked rice. If you are cooking the rice from scratch you will need about 75g/3oz rice to produce 150g/5oz cooked rice.

The dough can also be made and baked on basic programme to make a simple loaf.

Yogurt and Bacon Rolls

Add the bacon and onion before the end of kneading.

Divide the dough into 8 and shape into balls.

Tip

The dough can also be baked on basic programme to make a simple loaf. Add the bacon and onion when machine bleeps for extra ingredients, or 5 minutes before the end of kneading.

These soft savoury rolls can be served with butter or a cream cheese filling for a fabulous snack. They are also delicious served with soups, particularly tomato, chicken or celery.

Remove the bread pan from the machine. Pour in the water. Add the yogurt, egg, butter, sugar and salt. Add the flour, making sure that the liquid is completely covered. Sprinkle the yeast over the flour. If your machine recommends that you add the dry ingredients first, simply reverse the order that you add them to the pan.

Fit the bread pan in the machine, set the programme to the dough setting and press start.

Meanwhile, cook the bacon in a heavy-based frying pan. When the fat begins to run, add the onion and continue to cook until the bacon is done and the onions begin to colour.

When the machine beeps for extra ingredients, or about 5 minutes before the end of kneading, add the bacon and onion.

When the cycle has finished, transfer the dough to a lightly floured work surface. Knock back and lightly knead.

Ingredients
4 tbsp water
6 tbsp natural yogurt
1 egg
50g/2oz butter
2 tbsp caster sugar
1 tsp salt
375g/13oz strong white bread flour
1 tsp fast-acting dried yeast

To complete:
175g/6oz thick-cut back bacon
1 small onion, finely chopped
milk to glaze

Divide the dough into 8 equal pieces and shape into round balls. Place on a greased baking sheet, allowing enough space for the rolls to expand. Cover loosely and allow to rise until doubled in size.

Carefully brush with a little milk to glaze. Cook in a preheated oven at 200°C/400°F/gas mark 6 for 15 to 20 minutes until the rolls are golden and sound hollow when tapped. Transfer to a wire rack to cool.

Beef Braid

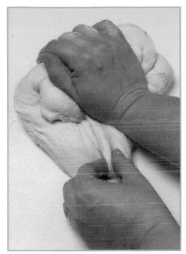

Knock back and knead the dough.

Remove the bread pan from the machine. Pour in the water. Add the oil, sugar and salt. Add the flour, making sure that the water is completely covered. Place the milk powder in one corner. Sprinkle the yeast over the flour. If your machine recommends that you add the dry ingredients first, simply reverse the order that you add them to the pan.

Fit the bread pan in the machine, set the programme to the dough setting and press start.

Meanwhile, make the beef filling. Place the beef, onion and garlic in

Ingredients
240ml/8¼ oz water
2 tbsp olive oil
1 tbsp sugar
1½ tsp salt
450g/1lb strong white
  bread flour
2 tbsp dried milk powder
1 tsp fast-acting dried yeast

To complete:
350g/12oz lean minced
  beef
1 onion, chopped
2 cloves garlic, chopped
2 tbsp brown fruity sauce
1 tsp dried mixed herbs
salt and freshly ground
  black pepper

Roll out dough into a rectangle 38 x25cm/15 x 10in.

a saucepan and cook over a medium heat until the mince is browned. Break up the meat as it cooks with the side of a spoon. Stir in the brown sauce and dried herbs, and season to taste. Allow to cool. Grease a large baking sheet.

When the cycle has finished, transfer the dough to a lightly floured work surface. Knock back and lightly

Spread the meat filling down the centre of the dough.

knead. Roll out to a rectangle about 38 x 25cm/15 x 10in and carefully transfer to the baking sheet.

Spread the meat filling down the centre of the dough. With a sharp knife cut 10 strips at an angle either side of the filling, stopping just short of the filling.

Fold over one end and then fold the dough strips over the filling from alternate sides, tucking any excess dough underneath the end.

Cover loosely and leave in a warm place to rise for 30 minutes. Preheat the oven to 190°C/375°F/gas mark 5. Bake until golden brown – about 30 minutes. Serve hot or cold.

Fold the strips of dough over the filling.

Roast Vegetable Pizza

To make the base, remove the bread pan from the machine. Pour in the water. Add the oil, sugar and salt. Add the flour, making sure that the water is completely covered. Sprinkle the yeast over the flour. If your machine recommends that you add the dry ingredients first, simply reverse the order that you add them to the pan.

Fit the bread pan in the machine, set the programme to the dough setting and press start.

Meanwhile, preheat the oven to

Ingredients

Base:
120ml/4½fl oz water
1 tbsp olive oil
1 tsp sugar
½ tsp salt
250g/9oz strong white
   bread flour
1 tsp fast-acting dried yeast

Topping:
1 small red onion, cut into
   thin wedges
1 red pepper, seeded and
   cut into chunks
½ small aubergine, sliced
2 tbsp olive oil
1 clove garlic, sliced
salt and freshly ground
   black pepper
2 tbsp sun-dried tomato
   paste
2 plum tomatoes, seeded
   and cut into quarters
150g/5oz mozzarella
   cheese, sliced

caption in this space

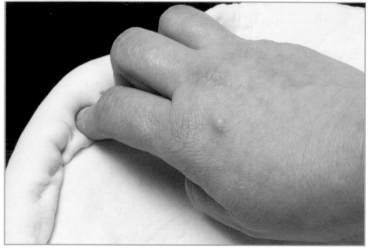

Fold the edges of the dough over to form a raised edge.

Spread the tomato paste over the dough and scatter the roasted vegetable on top. Add the tomatoes and cheese. Bake in the oven for 20 to 25 minutes until the base is crisp and golden.

Arrange vagetables and cheese on the pizza base.

200°C/400°F/gas mark 6. Place the onion, pepper and aubergine in a single layer on a baking sheet and drizzle with the oil. Scatter over the garlic slices and season with salt and pepper. Roast for 20 minutes until just softened.

When the dough cycle has finished, transfer the dough to a lightly floured work surface. Knock back and lightly knead. Roll the dough out to form a large circle. Place on a lightly greased baking sheet. Fold the edges of the dough over and push into the dough to form a raised edge.

Cinnamon Curl

This loaf hides a sweet, spicy filling.

Remove the bread pan from the machine. Pour in the milk. Add the egg, butter, sugar and salt. Add the flour, making sure that the liquid is completely covered. Sprinkle the yeast over the flour. If your machine recommends that you add the dry ingredients first, simply reverse the order that you add them to the pan.

Fit the bread pan in the machine, set the programme to the dough setting and press start.

When the cycle has finished, transfer the dough to a lightly floured work surface. Knock back and lightly knead.

Ingredients
175ml/6fl oz milk
1 egg
100g/4oz butter
100g/4oz caster sugar
½ tsp salt
450g/1lb strong white
  bread flour
1½ tsp fast acting dried yeast

To complete:
4 tbsp soured cream
4 tbsp demerara sugar
4 tbsp light muscovado
  sugar
1 tbsp ground cinnamon
1 tsp grated nutmeg
100g/4oz sultanas
beaten egg yolk to glaze.

Roll the dough into a rectangle.

Roll out the dough to form a rectangle 45 x 30cm/18 x 12in. Combine the soured cream, sugars, cinnamon, nutmeg and sultanas, and spread over the dough to within 2.5cm/1in of the edges. Roll up from the longest end and pinch the ends together to seal. Place on a lightly greased baking dish, seam-side down, and shape the roll into a loose spiral. Cover loosely and leave it to prove until doubled in size.

Push a skewer through the bread to prevent the spiral from uncurling during baking. Preheat the oven to 180°C/350°F/gas mark 4. Brush with beaten egg yolk and sprinkle with a little demerara sugar. Bake for about 30 minutes, or until the loaf sounds hollow when tapped underneath. Transfer to a wire rack to cool.

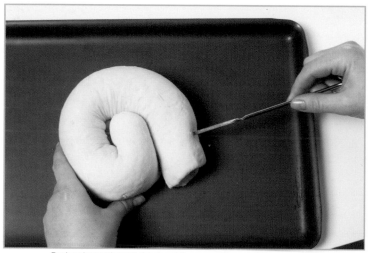

Push a skewer through the dough to prevent the spiral from uncurling.

Maple and Pecan Plait

Adding maple syrup.

An attractive, sweet loaf.

Remove the bread pan from the machine. Pour in the milk, soured cream and egg. Add the butter, maple syrup and salt. Add the flour, making sure that the liquid is completely covered. Sprinkle the yeast over the flour. If your machine recommends that you add the dry ingredients first, simply reverse the order that you add them to the pan.

Fit the bread pan in the machine, set the programme to the dough setting and press start. When the machine beeps for extra ingredients, or about 5 minutes before the end of kneading, add the pecan nuts to the pan.

When the cycle has finished, transfer the dough to a lightly floured work surface. Knock back and lightly knead.

Divide the dough into three equal pieces and roll to form ropes about 30cm/12in long. Pinch the three ropes together at one end and then plait them together. Tuck the ends underneath the bread to secure and place on a lightly greased baking sheet. Cover loosely and leave in a warm place until doubled in size.

Bake in a preheated oven at 200°C/400°F/gas mark 6 for 30 to 35 minutes, or until golden and the loaf sounds hollow when tapped underneath.

Transfer to a wire rack and brush the top with maple syrup while the plait is still hot. Sprinkle a few pecans on top and allow to cool.

Ingredients
100ml/4fl oz milk
142ml/5fl oz carton soured cream
1 egg
25g/1oz butter
5 tbsp maple syrup
½ tsp salt
450g/1lb strong white bread flour
1½ tsp fast-acting dried yeast
100g/4oz pecan nuts, chopped

To complete:
maple syrup
chopped pecan nuts to sprinkle

Plait the strands of bread.

Marmalade Butterfly Roll

Knock back the dough.

Remove the bread pan from the machine. Pour in the water. Add the butter, sugar and salt. Add the flour, making sure that the water is completely covered. Sprinkle the yeast over the flour. If your machine recommends that you add the dry ingredients first, simply reverse the order that you add them to the pan.

Fit the bread pan in the machine, set the programme to the dough setting and press start.

When the dough cycle has finished, transfer the dough to a lightly floured work surface. Knock back and lightly knead. Roll out the dough to form a 30cm/12in square. Brush the surface with melted butter, spread the marmalade over the dough and then sprinkle with the ground almonds. Roll up tightly from one short end, until you reach the middle of the dough. Roll up the dough from the other end in the same way until the rolls meet in the middle. Turn over and place joint side down on a baking sheet. Brush the top with melted butter.

Cover loosely and leave in a warm place until doubled in size. Bake in a preheated oven at 190°C/375°F/gas mark 5 for 25 to 30 minutes, or until golden and the loaf sounds hollow when tapped underneath. Transfer to a wire rack to cool.

Mix the icing sugar and orange juice together and drizzle over the loaf. Allow to set before serving.

Ingredients

140ml/4½fl oz water
25g/1oz butter
2 tbsp light muscovado sugar
½ tsp salt
300g/10½oz strong white bread flour
½ tsp fast-acting dried yeast

To complete:

25g/1oz butter, melted
6 tbsp orange marmalade
4 tbsp ground almonds
50g/2oz icing sugar
1 tsp orange juice

Roll up from an end to the middle, then roll from the other end.

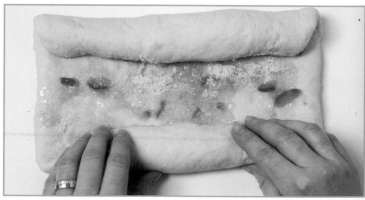

Apricot and Almond Ring

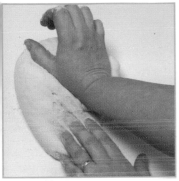

Knock back the dough and knead.

reverse the order that you add them to the pan.

Fit the bread pan in the machine and set the programme to the dough setting.

When the cycle has finished, transfer the dough to a lightly floured work surface.

Beat the apricots, almonds, sugar, butter, orange juice and zest together until well combined.

Ingredients
100ml/4fl oz milk
1 egg
25g/1oz butter
50g/2oz caster sugar
½ tsp salt
300g/10½oz strong white
   bread flour
1 tsp fast acting dried yeast

To complete:
50g/2oz ready to eat dried
   apricots, chopped
50g/2oz ground almonds
25g/1oz light muscovado
   sugar
25g/1oz butter, melted
grated zest and juice of
   orange

Spoon mixture into the middle of the dough.

Remove the bread pan from the machine. Pour in the milk. Add the egg, butter, caster sugar and salt. Add the flour, making sure that the liquid is completely covered. Sprinkle the yeast over the flour. If your machine recommends that you add the dry ingredients first, simply

When the dough is ready, turn out onto a lightly floured surface and lightly knead. Take two-thirds of the dough and roll it into a rope. Press out to flatten and use it to line the base and a little way up the side of a 20cm/8in ring tin. Spoon the apricot mixture in a circle into the middle of

the dough. Flatten remaining dough into a long length and use to cover the apricot mixture pressing it gently down the sides to seal. Cover loosely and leave in a warm place to rise until almost doubled in size.

Bake in preheated oven 190°C/ 375°F/gas mark 5 for 30 to 35 mins, until golden and cooked through. Transfer to a wire rack to cool.

149

Lemon Cardamom and Pistachio Nut Bread

Adding pistachio nuts.

A semi-sweet bread that is delicious served spread with lemon curd.

Remove the bread pan from the machine. Pour in the milk, lemon juice and zest. Add the egg, butter, sugar and salt. Add the flour, making sure that the water is completely covered. Crush the cardamom pods and remove the seeds. Add them to the pan and sprinkle yeast over the flour. If your machine recommends you add the dry ingredients first, simply reverse the order that you add them to the pan.

Fit the bread pan in the machine, set the programme to the dough setting and press start. When the machine beeps for extra ingredients,

or about 5 minutes before the end of kneading, add the pistachio nuts

When the cycle has finished, transfer the dough to a lightly floured work surface. Knock back and lightly knead.

Divide the dough into six pieces and roll each into a slightly elongated round. Place them in a line in a lightly greased 23 x 13cm/ 9 x 5in loaf tin. Cover loosely and allow to rise in a warm place until doubled in size. Bake in a preheated oven at 180°C/350°F/gas mark 4 for 35 to 40 minutes, or until the bread sounds hollow when tapped underneath. Remove the loaf from the tin and transfer to a wire rack to cool completely. Dissolve the icing sugar in the lemon juice and brush over the bread while it is still warm.

Ingredients

75ml/3fl oz milk
grated zest and juice of
  1 lemon
1 egg
50g/2oz butter
50g/2oz caster sugar
½ tsp salt
350g/12oz strong white
  bread flour
8 cardamom pods
1 tsp fast-acting dried yeast
50g/2oz pistachio nuts

To complete:

1 tbsp lemon juice
1 tbsp icing sugar

Divide the dough into 6 and place in a lightly greased loaf tin.

Bara Brith

Add fruit towards the end of kneading.

Knock back dough and shape.

Ingredients
150ml/5fl oz milk

1 egg

25g/1oz butter

1 tbsp light muscovado
  sugar

1 tsp salt

325g/11oz strong white
  bread flour

1 tsp mixed spice

1½ tsp fast-acting dried yeast

150g/5oz currants

100g/4oz sultanas

50g/2oz mixed peel

To glaze:
Honey

This Welsh bread is packed with fruit. The name means speckled bread and that is just what it is. Most of the sweetness of the bread comes from the fruit.

Remove the bread pan from the machine. Pour in the milk. Add the egg, butter, sugar and salt. Add the flour, making sure that the liquid is completely covered. Add the mixed spice and sprinkle the yeast over the flour. If your machine recommends that you add the dry ingredients first, simply reverse the order that you add them to the pan.

Fit the bread pan in the machine, set the programme to the dough setting. When the machine beeps for extra ingredients, or about 5 minutes before the end of kneading, add the dried fruit to the pan.

When the cycle has finished, transfer the dough to a lightly floured work surface. Knock back and lightly knead. Shape the dough into a round and place it on a lightly greased baking tray. Cover loosely and leave it to prove in a warm place, until doubled in size.

Bake in the centre of a preheated oven at 180°C/350°F/gas mark 4 for 35 minutes until golden and cooked through.

Transfer to a wire rack and brush with honey while it is still hot. Allow to cool.

Tip
Bara Brith has a very high proportion of fruit and you will need to add this to the dough manually even if your machine has a fruit and nut dispenser, as they will not fit in the compartment.

Cranberry and Walnut Loaf

You will have to think ahead when making this loaf because you need to make a "sponge" starter 12 to 24 hours before you start to make the bread. However, the light, airy texture and fabulous taste of this semi-sweet bread is well worth the extra effort.

Place the milk in a small saucepan and heat until almost boiling. Stir in the sugar and remove from the heat. Add the water. Allow to cool slightly until the liquid is just tepid. Place the flour and yeast in a large bowl and stir until combined. Stir in the milk mixture. Do not worry if the mixture is lumpy; it does not need to be smooth. Cover with a tea towel and leave in a warm place for between 12 and 24 hours.

Remove the bread pan from the machine. Pour in the sponge and add the water. Add the oil, honey and salt. Add the flour, making sure that the liquid is completely covered. Add the walnuts and

Ingredients

Sponge:
75ml/3fl oz milk
1 tsp caster sugar
75ml/3fl oz water
125g/4½oz strong white
   bread flour
1 tsp fast-acting dried yeast

Bread:
200ml/7fl oz water
2 tbsp walnut oil
2 tbsp honey
1 tsp salt
450g/1lb strong white
   bread flour
1 tsp yeast
100g/4oz walnuts,
   chopped
75g/3oz dried cranberries
beaten egg, or milk

Pour the sponge into the bread pan.

Shape the dough into a round loaf.

Brush with beaten egg to glaze.

sprinkle the yeast over the flour. If your machine recommends that you add the dry ingredients first, simply reverse the order that you add them to the pan.

Fit the bread pan in the machine, set the programme to dough setting and press start. When the machine beeps for extra ingredients, or about 5 minutes before the end of kneading, add the cranberries to the pan.

When the dough cycle has finished, transfer the dough to a lightly floured work surface. Knock back and lightly knead. Shape the dough into a round loaf and place it on a lightly greased baking tray.

Cover loosely with oiled cling wrap and leave in a warm place to rise until doubled in size. Brush with beaten egg or milk to glaze. Take a very sharp knife and slash a large cross into the top of the loaf. Bake in a preheated oven at 200°C/ 400°F/gas mark 6 for about 35 minutes, until golden and the loaf sounds hollow when tapped underneath.

Transfer to a wire rack to cool.

Malted Fruit Buns

Best served warm or lightly toasted.

Remove the bread pan from the machine. Pour in the water. Add the butter, sugar, malt extract and salt. Add the flour, making sure that the water is completely covered. Add the mixed spice and place the milk powder in one corner. Sprinkle the yeast over the flour. If your machine recommends that you add the dry ingredients first, simply reverse the order that you add them to the pan.

Ingredients
240ml/8½fl oz water
25g/1oz butter
4 tbsp light muscovado
  sugar
2 tbsp malt extract
1 tsp salt
450g/1lb strong white
  bread flour
2 tsp mixed spice
2 tbsp dried milk powder
1 tsp fast-acting dried yeast
150g/5oz mixed dried fruit

To glaze:
2 tbsp milk
2 tbsp caster sugar

Add the mixed fruit to the pan.

Brush with glaze while still hot.

Fit the bread pan in the machine, set the programme to the dough setting and press start. When the machine beeps for extra ingredients, or about 5 minutes before the end of kneading, add the mixed dried fruit to the pan.

When the cycle has finished, transfer the dough to a lightly floured work surface. Knock back and lightly knead. Divide the dough into 8 equal-sized pieces and then roll each into a ball. Place the buns on a lightly greased baking sheet, allowing enough space for them to rise and expand. Cover the buns loosely and leave them to prove in a warm place.

When the buns have almost doubled in size, remove the cling wrap and bake them in the centre of a preheated oven at 200°C/400°F/gas mark 6 for 15 to 20 minutes until golden and cooked through. While the buns are cooking, put the sugar and milk in a small saucepan and heat, stirring until the sugar dissolves.

Transfer the cooked buns to a wire rack to cool. Brush the glaze over the buns while they are still hot.

Iced Finger Buns

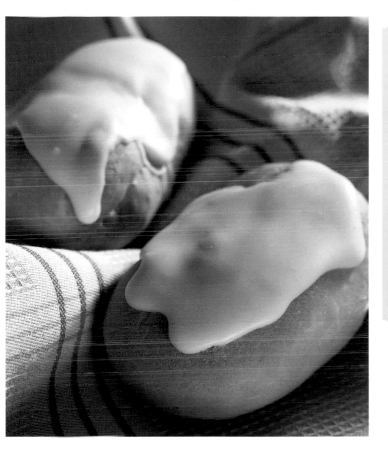

Ingredients

120ml/4fl oz milk
120ml/4fl oz soured cream
1 egg
25g/1oz butter
1½ tsp vanilla extract
2 tbsp light muscovado
    sugar
1 tsp salt
450g/1lb strong white
    bread flour
1½ tsp fast-acting dried yeast

To complete:

100g/4oz icing sugar
1 to 2 tbsp water

Made with a fabulous sour-cream-enriched dough these buns will appeal to young and old alike. Remove the bread pan from the machine. Pour in the milk, soured cream and egg. Add the butter, vanilla extract, sugar and salt.

Add the flour, making sure that the water is completely covered. Sprinkle the yeast over the flour. If your machine recommends that you add the dry ingredients first, simply reverse the order that you add them to the pan.

Pour in the milk and soured cream.

When the buns have almost doubled in size, remove the cling wrap and bake them in the centre of a preheated oven at 200°C/400°F/ gas mark 6 for 15 to 20 minutes until golden and cooked through.

When the buns are cool, sift the icing sugar into a small mixing bowl and stir in the water to form smooth icing. Spread the icing along the top of each bun and allow to set.

Fit the bread pan in the machine, set the programme to the dough setting and press start. When the cycle has finished, transfer the dough to a lightly floured work surface. Knock back and lightly knead.

Divide the dough into 10 equal-sized pieces and then roll each into a ball. Roll the ball into a sausage shape about 7.5cm/3in long. Place buns on a lightly greased baking tray, allowing enough space for them to rise and expand. Cover the buns with a piece of oiled cling wrap and leave them to prove in a warm place.

Spread icing on buns and allow to set.

Honey Buns

Sweet and sticky, these honey-flavoured buns are a real treat

Remove the bread pan from the machine. Pour in the milk. Add the egg, butter, honey and salt. Add the flour, making sure that the liquid is completely covered. Sprinkle the yeast over the flour. If your machine recommends that you add the dry ingredients first, simply reverse the order that you add them to the pan.

Fit the bread pan in the machine, set the programme to the dough setting and press start.

Ingredients

100ml/4fl oz milk
1 egg
25g/1oz butter
50g/2oz thick honey
½ tsp salt
300g/10½oz strong white
  bread flour
1 tsp fast-acting dried yeast

To complete:

75g/3oz butter, softened
6 tbsp thick honey
1 tbsp demerara sugar

Break eggs into the pan.

Place each piece into a muffin cup.

When the cycle has finished, transfer the dough to a lightly floured work surface. Knock back and lightly knead. Roll out the dough to form a rectangle about 30 x 25cm/12 x 10in. Beat the softened butter, honey and sugar until well combined. Spread about two-thirds of the honey mixture over the dough, leaving a 2.5cm/1in border on one of the long sides. Roll up tightly from the other long side, like a Swiss roll. Cut into 12 equal pieces and place each in a greased muffin cup.

Spoon a little of the remaining honey mixture onto the top of each bun. Cover loosely and place in a warm place until almost doubled in size.

Bake in a preheated oven at 180°C/350°F/gas mark 4 for 20 minutes until golden. Allow to cool in the tin for about 5 minutes, before turning out onto a wire rack to cool completely.

Cinnamon Ring Doughnuts

These doughnuts will keep in an airtight container for a day or two but are sure to disappear fast. They are best eaten warm. Eat straight away, or warm through for 10 minutes in a medium oven or for a few seconds in the microwave.

Remove the bread pan from the machine. Pour in the milk. Add the egg, butter, sugar and salt. Add the flour, making sure that the liquid is completely covered. Sprinkle the spices and yeast over the flour. If your machine recommends that

you add the dry ingredients first, simply reverse the order that you add them to the pan.

Fit the bread pan in the machine, set the programme to the dough setting and press start. When the cycle has finished, transfer the dough to a lightly floured work surface. Knock back and lightly knead.

Roll the dough out to a thickness of about 7.5mm/1/3in. Cut out rings, using a 7.5cm/3in and a 3cm/1½in biscuit cutter. Place the rings on

Ingredients
150ml/5fl oz milk
1 egg
50g/2oz butter
2 tbsp caster sugar
½ tsp salt
450g/1lb strong white
    bread flour
½ tsp ground cinnamon
¼ tsp ground nutmeg
1½ tsp fast-acting dried yeast

To complete:
3 tbsp caster sugar
1 tbsp ground cinnamon
oil for deep-frying

Cut out doughnut rings with biscuit cutters.

a lightly greased baking tray, cover loosely and leave to prove for about 30 minutes in a warm place.

Mix together the caster sugar and cinnamon and spread out on a plate. Line another baking sheet with kitchen paper.

Heat the oil in a deep-fat fryer to 180°C/350°F and deep-fry the doughnuts 3 or 4 at a time for about 3 minutes, turning once until golden. Remove with a draining spoon and drain briefly on the kitchen paper. Toss in the caster sugar mixture and serve.

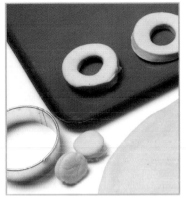
Cut out the rings and place on a baking tray.

Deep-fry in batches.

Toss doughnuts in cinnamon sugar to coat.

Marzipan and Almond Croissants

These delicious French pastries taste fantastic but you will need to prepare ahead because they require a lot of rolling and chilling. However, you could make the croissants up the day before, chill them in the refrigerator overnight and bake

Dot one portion of butter over two-thirds of the dough.

Fold uncovered dough over butter and refold.

them fresh in the morning. You can also freeze the uncooked croissants, thaw for about 2 hours and bake them when required.

Remove the bread pan from the machine. Pour in the water. Add the egg, butter, sugar and salt. Add the flour, making sure that the water is completely covered. Sprinkle the yeast over the flour. If your machine recommends that you add the dry ingredients first, simply reverse the order that you add them to the pan.

Fit the bread pan in the machine, set the programme to the dough setting and press start.

When the cycle has finished, transfer the dough to a lightly floured work surface. Knock back and lightly knead. Roll out the dough to form a rectangle about 40 x 20cm/16 x 8in.

Divide the butter into three portions. Dot one portion over two-thirds of the dough, leaving a border around the edges. Fold the dough into three by folding the plain part over first and covering with the other third. Seal the edges by pressing

Ingredients
200ml/7fl oz water
1 egg
25g/1oz butter
50g/2oz caster sugar
1 tsp salt
450g/1lb strong white
   bread flour
1 tsp fast-acting dried yeast

To complete:
250g/9oz unsalted butter,
   at room temperature
225g/8oz marzipan
beaten egg to glaze
flaked almonds, to sprinkle
icing sugar to dust

them with a rolling pin. Give the dough a quarter turn and repeat the rolling and the folding without the butter. Cover and chill for 30 minutes.

Repeat the rolling. Fold once with butter and again without. Chill for 20 minutes. Repeat again with the remaining butter. Fold and roll twice more without butter and chill for 30 minutes.

Roll the dough into a rectangle about 45 x 30cm/18 x 12in and trim the edges. Cut the rectangle into six squares and then diagonally across to make 12 triangles. Brush with beaten egg.

Grate the marzipan and sprinkle over the dough triangles. Starting at the longest edge of one triangle, loosely roll up, finishing with the tip tucked underneath. Place in a curved crescent shape on a lightly greased baking tray. Repeat with the remaining dough, leaving space for the croissants to spread.

Sprinkle grated marzipan over the dough triangles.

Brush with beaten egg and sprinkle with a few flaked almonds. Cover loosely with oiled cling wrap and leave to prove in a warm place for 30 minutes. Preheat the oven to 220°C/425°F/gas mark 7 and bake for 20 to 25 minutes until golden brown. Transfer to a wire rack and allow to cool. Dust with icing sugar to serve.

Roll dough up from the long end and then curve into a crescent shape.

Apple Danish

Remove the bread pan from the machine. Pour in the milk. Add the egg, butter, sugar and salt. Add the flour, making sure that the liquid is completely covered. Sprinkle the yeast over the flour. If your machine recommends that you add the dry ingredients first, simply reverse the order that you add them to the pan.

Fit the bread pan in the machine, set the programme to the dough setting and press start.

Place150g/5oz of the butter between 2 sheets of greaseproof paper. Using a rolling pin, beat the butter into a rectangle about 18 x 7.5cm/7 x 3in.

When the dough cycle has

Ingredients
120ml/4½fl oz milk
2 eggs
25g/1oz butter
1 tsp sugar
½ tsp salt
350g/12oz strong white
   bread flour
1 tsp fast-acting dried yeast

To complete:
175g/6oz butter
2 Bramley cooking apples,
   peeled, cored and
   chopped
25g/1oz sultanas
2 tbsp demerara sugar
¼ tsp freshly grated nutmeg
grated zest ½ orange
beaten egg to glaze
honey to drizzle

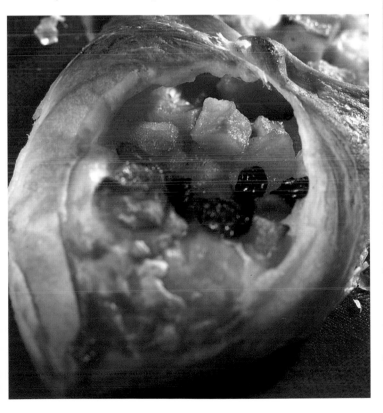

finished, transfer the dough to a lightly floured work surface. Knock back and lightly knead. Roll out the dough into a rectangle about 30 x 20cm/12 x 8in. Place the butter in the centre of the dough and fold over the ends, sealing the edges. Give the dough a quarter turn.

Roll the butter between two sheets of greaseproof paper.

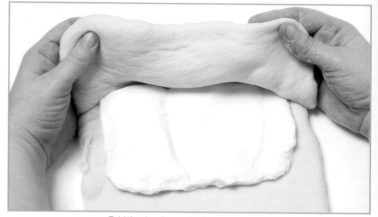

Fold the dough over the butter to enclose.

Roll out to form a rectangle about 30 x 20cm/12 x 8in and fold into three. Cover and chill for 30 minutes. Repeat the rolling and folding process twice more and chill again.

Place the remaining butter in a small pan and heat until melted. Add the apple, sultanas, nutmeg and orange zest. Cook gently for 5 minutes until the apple begins to soften.

Roll out the dough to form a 40cm/16in square and cut into 16 equal-sized squares. Place the squares onto lightly greased baking trays. Place a little of the apple mixture diagonally across each square. Bring the two uncovered corners of dough across the filling to meet in the middle, and pinch to seal them together.

Cover loosely and allow to prove for 30 minutes. Preheat the oven to

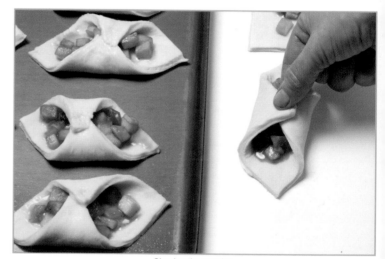

Shaping the pastries.

180°C/350°F/gas mark 4. Brush the pastry with beaten egg and bake for 15 to 20 minutes. Transfer to a wire rack and drizzle with a little honey. Allow to cool.

Sourdough-style Breads

Because these breads use commercial yeast to get the starter going, purists would not call them sourdough breads. However, they are made in the same style and the fermented starter gives the bread a similar texture and flavour. While you can bake sourdough in a bread machine, the nature of the starter can be a little unpredictable, so I prefer to bake the bread in the oven. I have made sourdough in a machine, only to find the starter was so active that the bread hit the top of the machine. Making the dough only in the machine also means that the second rising can be done at a lower temperature, which will further improve the texture of the bread.

Adding a little extra yeast to the dough, while not absolutely necessary, helps ensure that you get a successful loaf each time, with the minimum of effort. But feel free to omit it if you know your starter is very active and bubbly. Once you have made the starter, it can be replenished and kept in the refrigerator almost indefinitely, ready to make more bread loaf in the future. However, if your starter begins to turn pink or develops a mould, discard it and start again.

Some breads use a sponge starter. They are made fresh each time and left to develop for varying length of times – the

French "poolish" ferments for at least 2 hours to give a less yeasty flavour and the Italian "biga" is left for around 12 hours. Each gives these rustic breads their unique characteristics. I am sure that once you have tried these breads, you will agree that their character and fabulous flavour make them well worth any extra effort required.

Sourdough-style Starter

Combine the flour and yeast in a large bowl. Stir in the water until combined. Cover with a clean tea towel and allow to stand in a warm place for 3 to 5 days. The mixture will begin to bubble in a few minutes and then will froth up to at least double its size. However, after a while it will settle down. When the mixture has a sour, yeasty aroma it is ready to use. Stir the mixture well and store in a covered jar in the refrigerator.

To use your starter and keep it going

When required, remove the starter from the refrigerator and bring back to room temperature. Remove the amount needed for the recipe and replenish the starter with equal amounts of flour and water. I find that it is easier to use a cup measure for this. Use the cup that comes with the machine. If you take 1 cup of starter, replace it with 1 cup of water and 1 cup of flour. Stir until well combined. Allow the yeast to bubble and grow again before returning the starter to the refrigerator. The cold temperature will slow the yeast's activity right down. Occasionally use milk in place of the water, or add a little sugar to re-nourish the starter. There is no need to add extra yeast. If you do not use the starter to make bread you can keep it going by discarding some and replacing the amount with fresh flour and water. Do this at least once a week.

Ingredients
480ml/17fl oz water
300g/10½oz plain flour
2 tsp fast-acting dried yeast

White Sourdough Bread

Pouring in the starter.

Remove the bread pan from the machine. Pour the starter and water into the pan. Add the olive oil, sugar and salt. Add the flour, making sure that the liquid water is completely covered. Sprinkle the yeast over the flour. If your machine recommends that you add the dry ingredients first, simply reverse the order that you add them to the pan.

Fit the bread pan in the machine, set the programme to the dough setting and press start.

When the dough cycle has finished, transfer the dough to a lightly floured work surface.

Knock back and lightly knead. Shape the dough into a round loaf or a long loaf and place on a lightly greased baking tray.

Cover loosely and leave to rise until doubled in size. Sprinkle with flour. Take a very sharp knife and slash the loaf a few times. Sprinkle with a little more flour. Bake in a preheated oven at 220°C/425°F/gas mark 7 for about 30 to 35 minutes, until golden and the loaf sounds hollow when tapped underneath.

Transfer to a wire rack to cool.

Ingredients

240ml/8½fl oz (1 cup) sourdough starter (see page 173)

100ml/4fl oz water

2 tbsp olive oil

1 tbsp caster sugar

1 tsp salt

450g/1lb strong white bread flour

½ tsp fast-acting dried yeast

flour to sprinkle

An active starter.

Sourdough with Rye

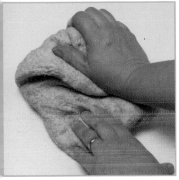

Knock back and knead the dough.

Remove the bread pan from the machine. Pour the starter and water into the pan. Add the olive oil, sugar and salt. Add the flours, making sure that the liquid is completely covered. Sprinkle the yeast over the flour. If your machine recommends that you add the dry ingredients first, simply reverse the order that you add them to the pan.

Fit the bread pan in the machine, set the programme to the dough setting and press start.

When the dough cycle has finished, transfer the dough to a lightly floured work surface. Knock back and lightly knead. Shape the dough into a round loaf or a long loaf and place on a lightly greased baking tray.

Cover loosely and leave in a warm place to rise until doubled in size. Sprinkle with flour. Take a very sharp knife and slash the loaf a few times. Sprinkle with a little more flour. Bake in a preheated oven at 220°C/425°F/ gas mark 7 for about 30 to 35 minutes, or until golden and the loaf sounds hollow when tapped underneath.

Transfer to a wire rack to cool.

Ingredients

240ml/8½fl oz (1 cup) sourdough starter (see page 173)

100ml/4fl oz water

2 tbsp olive oil

1 tbsp caster sugar

1 tsp salt

350g/12oz strong white bread flour

100g/4oz rye flour

½ tsp fast-acting dried yeast

flour to sprinkle

Adding the flours.

French Sticks

These are made with a sponge starter to give a more authentic texture and flavour – well worth the extra wait.

Place the flour in a bowl and stir in the yeast. Make a well in the centre and pour in the water. Mix until a wet, sticky dough is produced. Cover with a tea towel and leave in a warm place for between 2 and 4 hours. If you are not going to make the bread straight away, place the

Ingredients

Sponge:
350g/12oz strong white
  bread flour
2 tsp fast-acting dried yeast
300ml/10fl oz lukewarm
  water

Bread:
150ml/5fl oz water
1 tbsp olive oil
1 tsp salt
350g/12oz strong white
  bread flour
beaten egg to glaze

Place dough strands on a floured tea towel. Pull up the towel between the strands to prevent them expanding sideways.

Slash the sticks with a very sharp knife.

sponge into the refrigerator for up to 12 hours. Remove from the refrigerator about 30 minutes before progressing to allow the sponge to come back to room temperature.

Remove the bread pan from the machine. Pour in the sponge and add the water, oil and salt. Add the flour, making sure that the liquid is completely covered.

Fit the bread pan in the machine, set the programme to the dough setting and press start. Use a French or continental dough setting if available; they have a longer,

slower rise and will give even better results.

When the dough cycle has finished, transfer the dough to a lightly floured work surface. Knock back and lightly knead. Divide the dough into three. Roll each piece into a ball and then roll and pull it into a long, sausage shape.

Place a tea towel on a board and liberally sprinkle it with flour. Place the dough strands on the towel, pull the towel up between them and push them fairly close together. This will prevent them from expanding

outwards. Cover with another floured towel and leave in a warm place for about 1 hour.

Carefully transfer the sticks to a lightly greased baking sheet. Brush with beaten egg or milk to glaze. Take a very sharp knife and slash across the sticks a few times. Bake in a preheated oven at 200°C/400°F /gas mark 6 for about 35 minutes, until golden and the loaves sound hollow when tapped underneath.

Transfer to a wire rack to cool.

Italian Bread with Mozzarella and Roasted Vegetables

The sponge starter needs to be made well in advance for this rustic Italian-style bread. The dough can also be baked unfilled.

Place the milk in a small saucepan and heat until almost boiling. Stir in the sugar and remove from the heat. Add the water. Allow to cool slightly until the liquid is just tepid. Place the flour and yeast in a large bowl and stir until combined. Stir in the milk mixture. Do not worry if the mixture is lumpy; it does not need to be smooth. Cover with a tea towel and leave in a warm place for between 12 and 24 hours.

Remove the bread pan from the machine. Pour in the sponge and add the water. Add the olive oil, sugar and salt. Add the flour, making sure that the liquid is completely covered. Sprinkle the yeast over the flour. If your machine recommends that you add the dry ingredients

Add mozzarella and vegetables to dough.

Ingredients

Sponge:
75ml/3fl oz milk
1 tsp caster sugar
75ml/3fl oz water
125g/4½oz strong white
   bread flour
1 tsp fast-acting dried yeast

Bread:
200ml/7fl oz water
2 tbsp olive oil
1 tbsp caster sugar
1 tsp salt
450g/1lb strong white
   bread flour
1 tsp yeast

To complete:
1 red pepper, seeded and cut
   into bite-size pieces
1 red onion, peeled and cut
   into thin wedges
2 tbsp olive oil
1 clove garlic, chopped
150g/5oz mozzarella
   cheese, diced
flour to dust

first, simply reverse the order that you add them to the pan.

Fit the bread pan in the machine, set the programme to the dough setting and press start.

To make the filling, preheat the oven to 200°C/400°F/gas mark 6. Place the onion and pepper in a single layer on a baking sheet and drizzle with the oil. Scatter the garlic over them and roast for 30 minutes until just tender and beginning o char.

When the dough cycle has finished, transfer the dough to a lightly floured work. Knock back and lightly knead. Roll out the dough to form a rectangle about 45 x 30cm/18 x 12in. Place it long side towards you, and spread the roasted vegetable over two-thirds of the dough, leaving a 5cm/2in border. Scatter the cheese on top. Fold the uncovered dough over the vegetables. Then fold over the other end. Press the edges together to seal. Turn over, place on a lightly greased baking tray and press the ends together to seal in the filling.

Cover loosely and leave in a warm place to rise until doubled in size. Sprinkle flour over the top. Bake in a preheated oven at 220°C/425°F/gas mark 7 for 25 to 30 minutes, until golden and the loaf sounds hollow when tapped underneath.

Transfer to a wire rack to cool. Serve warm or cold.

CAKES

Many machines have a cake-making programme. This can vary considerably from machine to machine. Some will mix and bake cakes. With others you have to mix the cake by hand and then use the machine's bake programme to cook the cake. Some instruction manuals suggest pre-mixing the wet and dry ingredients in two separate bowls, then adding them to the machine for the final mixing. This creates rather a lot of washing up and, to my mind, defeats the point of using the machine. In all the models I used with a cake-mixing facility, I found that I obtained perfectly acceptable results by adding the liquid ingredients, followed by the dry ingredients, to the pan and then allowing the machine to do the rest. Baking time can vary from model to model, but once you are familiar with your machine you can increase or decrease the cooking time stated in the recipes as required.

The cake programme is not suitable for cakes that require a hot oven or for whisk sponges. Baking powder is the main raising agent.

Tip for successful cakes

- Add wet ingredients first.
- Butter or margarine must be very soft before it is added. Either soften by beating first or zap in the microwave for a few seconds to soften.
- About 10 minutes after the start of the programme, scrape down the sides of the pan with a rubber spatula, paying particular attention to the corners of the pan to ensure that all the ingredients are fully incorporated.
- If you are quick, you can remove the paddles at the start of the baking time to avoid holes in the cake. But take care as the surfaces will be getting hot!
- The pre-programmed bake cycle will vary from make to make, so check the cake about 10 minutes before the end of the cooking time to see if it is cooked.
- At the end of the cycle, increase the cooking time if the cake is not cooked. Use the bake-only programme to extend the cooking time. Note that this facility may not be available on budget machines. In this case, if the cake is not cooked, you will have to transfer it to a conventional oven and the resulting cake may be slightly sunken.
- When the cake is cooked, remove the pan from the machine, using oven gloves. Allow the cake to cool in the tin for 10 minutes before transferring it to a wire rack to cool completely.

Madeira Cake

Adding the flour.

Check the cake mixture 10 minutes before the end of the cycle to see if it is cooked; it should be springy to the touch and a skewer inserted into the centre should come out clean. Allow the cycle to complete, if required. Retest, extending the baking time if needed.

When the cake is cooked, switch off the machine. Using oven gloves, carefully remove the pan. Allow the cake to cool in the tin for 10 minutes before turning out to cool completely.

Ingredients

3 eggs
2 tbsp milk
1 tsp vanilla essence
175g/6oz soft margarine or
  butter, softened
175g/6oz golden caster
  sugar
225g/8oz self-raising flour
1 tsp baking powder

A classic plain cake that is ideal for an everyday treat.

Remove the bread pan from the machine. Add the ingredients for the cake to the pan in the order listed.

Fit the bread pan in the machine, set the programme to the cake setting and press start. After 10 minutes, scrape down the side of the pan with a rubber spatula. This will help to ensure that the cake is fully mixed.

If the machine does not have a mixing facility, place all the ingredients in a mixing bowl and beat with an electric whisk until smooth. Spoon into the tin and select the bake-only cycle for 50 minutes.

Scrape down the sides of the baking pan with a spatula.

Almond Madeira Cake

Ingredients
Cake:
2 tbsp amaretto liqueur
3 eggs
175g/6oz soft margarine or
  butter, softened
175g/6oz golden caster
  sugar
150g/5oz self raising flour
100g/4oz ground almonds
1 tsp baking powder

To complete:
100g/4oz icing sugar
1 to 2 tbsp water or
  amaretto liqueur
1 tbsp toasted flaked
  almonds

The amaretto liqueur adds an extra rich almond flavour. It is available in miniature bottles. If you do not wish to use it, add 2 tbsp milk and 1 tsp almond extract to the cake mixture instead.

Remove the bread pan from the machine. Add the ingredients for the cake to the pan in the order listed.

Fit the bread pan in the machine, set the programme to the cake setting and press start. After 10 minutes, scrape down the side of the tin with a rubber spatula. This will help to ensure that cake is fully mixed.

If the machine does not have a mixing facility, place all the

191

Adding sugar.

cake to cool in the tin for 10 minutes before turning out onto a wire rack to cool completely.

To decorate, sift the icing sugar into a mixing bowl and add enough water or amaretto to mix to a smooth icing. Spread icing over the top of the cake and scatter the toasted flaked almonds.

Mix amaretto and icing sugar until smooth.

ingredients in a mixing bowl and beat with an electric whisk until combined. Spoon the mixture into the tin and select the bake-only cycle for 50 minutes.

Check the cake mixture 10 minutes before the end of the cycle to see if it is cooked; it should be springy to the touch. If you insert a skewer into the centre it should come out clean. Allow the cycle to complete, if required. Retest, extending baking time if needed.

When the cake is cooked, switch off the machine. Using oven gloves, carefully remove the pan. Allow the

Lemon Crunch Cake

This cake is one of the most popular cakes I know. There are many variations, but I found this simple to produce in the bread machine. The tart, lemon topping contrasts well with the sweetness of the cake.

Remove the bread pan from the machine. Add the ingredients for the cake in the order listed.

Fit the bread pan in the machine, set the programme to the cake setting, and press start. After 10 minutes, scrape down the side of the tin with a rubber spatula. This will help to ensure that the cake is fully mixed.

If the machine does not have a mixing facility, place all the ingredients in a mixing bowl and beat with an electric whisk until smooth. Spoon into the tin and select the bake-only cycle for 50 minutes.

Check the cake mixture 10 minutes before the end of the cycle to see if it is cooked; it should be

Ingredients
Cake:
3 eggs
grated zest and juice
  1 lemon
175g/6oz soft margarine or
  butter, softened
175g/6oz golden caster
  sugar
225g/8oz self-raising flour
1 tsp baking powder

To complete:
50g/2oz granulated sugar
juice 1 lemon

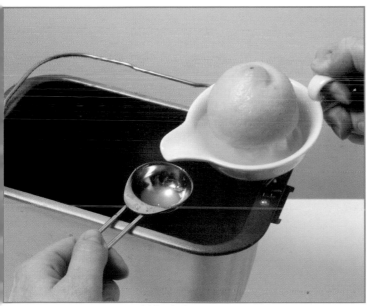

Adding the lemon juice.

springy to the touch and a skewer inserted into the centre should come out clean. Allow the cycle to complete, if required. Retest, extending baking time if needed.

When the cake is cooked, switch off the machine. Using oven gloves, carefully remove the pan. Allow the cake to cool in the tin for 10 minutes before turning out onto a wire rack.

Mix the granulated sugar and lemon juice together. Pierce the top of the cake several times with a skewer. Carefully spoon the lemon and sugar mixture over the hot cake, so that some soaks into the cake and some drizzles down the sides. Cool completely.

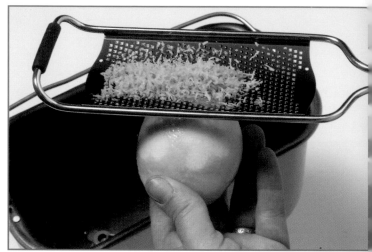

Grating the zest of the lemon.

Spoon the lemon and sugar mixture over the hot cake.

Seedy Cake

Adding the flour.

Adding the seeds.

Ingredients

3 eggs

2 tbsp orange or lemon juice

175g/6oz soft margarine or butter, softened

175g/6oz golden caster sugar

225g/8oz self raising flour

1 tsp baking powder

1 tbsp caraway or poppy seeds

An old-fashioned cake that is still a favourite.

Remove the bread pan from the machine. Add the ingredients for the cake to the pan in the order listed.

Fit the bread pan in the machine, set the programme to the cake setting and press start. After 10 minutes, scrape down the side of the tin with a rubber spatula. This will help to ensure that the cake is fully mixed. If the machine does not have a mixing facility, place all the ingredients in a mixing bowl and beat with an electric whisk until combined. Spoon into the tin and select the bake-only cycle for 50 minutes.

Check the cake mixture 10 minutes before the end of the cycle to see if it is cooked; it should be springy to the touch and a skewer inserted into the centre should come out clean. Allow the cycle to complete, if required. Retest, extending baking time if needed.

When the cake is cooked, switch off the machine. Using oven gloves, carefully remove the pan. Allow the cake to cool in the tin for 10 minutes before turning out onto a wire rack to cool completely.

Coconut cake

Complete by icing the cake.

Ingredients

2 eggs

6 tbsp milk

1 tsp vanilla essence

100g/4oz soft margarine or
  butter, softened

100g/4oz golden caster
  sugar

175g/6oz self-raising flour

75g/3oz desiccated
  coconut

1 tsp baking powder

To complete:

100g/4oz icing sugar

1–2 tbsp water

1 tbsp desiccated coconut,
  toasted

Remove the bread pan from the machine. Add the ingredients for the cake to the pan in the order listed.

Fit the bread pan in the machine, set the programme to the cake setting and press start. After 10 minutes, scrape down the side of the tin with a rubber spatula. This will help to ensure that the cake is fully mixed.

If the machine does not have a mixing facility, place all the ingredients in a mixing bowl and beat with an electric whisk until smooth. Spoon into the tin and select the bake-only cycle for 50 minutes.

Check the cake mixture 10 minutes before the end of the cycle to see if it is cooked; it should be springy to the touch and a skewer inserted into the centre should come out clean. Allow the cycle to complete, if required. Retest, extending baking time if needed.

When the cake is cooked, switch off the machine. Using oven gloves, carefully remove the pan. Allow the cake to cool in the tin for 10 minutes before turning out to cool completely.

To decorate, sift the icing sugar into a mixing bowl and add enough water to mix to a smooth icing. Spread the icing over the top of the cake and scatter with the toasted coconut.

You will need two eggs.

Chocolate Chip and Hazelnut Cake

Adding the baking powder.

Ingredients
3 eggs
1 tsp vanilla essence
175g/6oz soft margarine or
  butter, softened
175g/6oz golden caster
  sugar
225g/8oz self-raising flour
1 tsp baking powder
100g/4oz chocolate chips
50g/2oz toasted hazelnuts,
  chopped

Remove the bread pan from the machine. Add the ingredients to the pan in the order listed.

Fit the bread pan in the machine, set the programme to the cake setting and press start. After 10 minutes, scrape down the side of the tin with a rubber spatula. This will help to ensure that the cake is fully mixed.

If the machine does not have a mixing facility, place all the ingredients, except the chocolate chips and hazelnuts, in a mixing bowl and beat with an electric whisk until smooth. Stir in the chocolate

Adding the butter.

carefully remove the pan. Allow the cake to cool in the tin for 10 minutes before turning out to cool completely.

Adding the chocolate chips.

chips and hazelnuts. Spoon into the tin and select the bake-only cycle for 50 minutes.

Check the cake mixture 10 minutes before the end of the cycle to see if it is cooked; it should be springy to the touch and a skewer inserted into the centre should come out clean. Allow the cycle to complete, if required. Retest, extending baking time if needed.

When the cake is cooked, switch off the machine. Using oven gloves,

Cherry and Almond

Ingredients
3 eggs

4 tbsp milk

1 tsp almond essence

175g/6oz soft margarine or
butter, softened

175g/6oz golden caster
sugar

150g/5oz self raising flour

100g/4oz ground almonds

1 tsp baking powder

75g/3oz glacé cherries,
halved

Remove the bread pan from the machine. Add the ingredients for the cake to the pan in the order listed.

Fit the bread pan in the machine, set the programme to the cake setting and press start. After 10 minutes scrape down the side of the tin with a rubber spatula. This will help to ensure that cake is fully mixed.

If the machine does not have a mixing facility, place all the ingredients (except the cherries) in a mixing bowl and beat with an electric whisk until smooth. Fold the cherries into the mixture and spoon into the tin. Select the bake-only cycle for 50 minutes.

Add the butter or margarine.

Check the cake mixture 10 minutes before the end of the cycle to see if it is cooked; it should be springy to the touch and a skewer inserted into the centre should come out clean. Allow the cycle to complete, if required. Retest, extending baking time if needed.

When the cake is cooked, switch off the machine. Using oven gloves, carefully remove the pan. Allow the cake to cool in the tin for 10 minutes before turning out to cool completely.

Blanched almonds.

Apricot and Raisin Cake

a cake that is perfect for lunch boxes or afternoon tea.

Heat the orange juice in a small pan and add the apricots and raisins. Allow to stand for 20 minutes.

Remove the bread pan from the machine. Add the soaked fruit and juice and the remaining ingredients for the cake to the pan in the order listed.

Ingredients
5 tbsp orange juice
100g/4oz raisins
100g/4oz no-soak, dried
   apricots, chopped
3 eggs
1 tsp vanilla essence
175g/6oz soft margarine or
   butter, softened
175g/6oz golden caster
   sugar
200g/7oz self-raising flour
1 tsp baking powder

Chopping the apricots.

Adding the butter.

Fit the bread pan in the machine, set the programme to the cake setting and press start. After 10 minutes scrape down the sides of the tin with a rubber spatula. This will help to ensure that the cake is fully mixed.

If the machine does not have a mixing facility, soak the apricots as above. Place the remaining ingredients in a mixing bowl and beat with an electric whisk until combined. Beat in the apricots and spoon the mixture into the tin. Select the bake-only cycle for 50 minutes.

Check the cake mixture 10 minutes before the end of the cycle to see if it is cooked; it should be springy to the touch and a skewer inserted into the centre should come out clean. Allow the cycle to complete, if required. Retest, extending baking time if needed.

When the cake is cooked, switch off the machine. Using oven gloves, carefully remove the pan. Allow the cake to cool in the tin for 10 minutes before turning out onto a wire rack to cool completely.

Real Ale Teacake

This fruit cake is quite special as the ale plumps up the fruit and adds extra flavour. It is fabulous served with a chunk of cheese.

Place the ale, fruit, sugar and butter in a saucepan and heat gently until just boiling. Simmer for 15 minutes and allow to cool.

Remove the bread pan from the machine. Add the boiled fruit, followed by the eggs, flour, baking powder and mixed spice.

Fit the bread pan in the machine, set the programme to the cake setting and press start. After 10 minutes scrape down the side of the pan with a rubber spatula. This will help to ensure that the cake is fully mixed.

If the machine does not have a mixing facility, beat the sugar, butter, eggs, flour, baking powder and spice with an electric whisk until smooth. Beat in the soaked fruit. Spoon the mixture into the tin and select the bake-only cycle for 50 minutes.

Ingredients
225ml/8fl oz real ale
350g/12oz mixed dried
  fruit
125g/4½oz demerara sugar
175g/6oz butter
3 eggs
250g/9oz self-raising flour
1 tsp baking powder
1 tbsp mixed spice

Carefully measure the ale.

Check the cake mixture 10 minutes before the end of the cycle to see if it is cooked; a skewer inserted into the centre should come out clean. Allow the cycle to complete, if required. Retest, extending baking time if needed.

When the cake is cooked, switch off the machine. Using oven gloves, carefully remove the pan. Allow the cake to cool in the tin for 10 minutes before turning out onto a wire rack to cool completely.

Adding sugar.

Scrape the sides of the pan to ensure even mixing.

Fruit Malt Cake

Add 2 eggs.

Adding sultanas.

Ingredients
175g/6oz barley malt syrup
150ml/5fl oz milk
2 eggs
250g/9oz plain wholemeal
  flour
100g/4oz plain flour
1 tsp baking powder
½ tsp bicarbonate of soda
250g/12oz sultanas

A cross between bread and cake, this malt cake is fabulous served spread with butter.

Remove the bread pan from the machine. Add the barley malt syrup, milk and eggs to the pan. Mix together the remaining ingredients and add to the pan.

Fit the bread pan in the machine, set the programme to the cake setting and press start. After 10 minutes scrape down the side of the tin with a rubber spatula. This will help to ensure that the cake is fully mixed.

If the machine does not have a mixing facility, mix the syrup, milk and eggs together until well combined. Mix the remaining ingredients together and beat into the syrup mixture until well combined. Spoon into the tin and select the bake-only cycle for 50 minutes.

Check the cake mixture 10 minutes before the end of the cycle to see if it is cooked; a skewer inserted into the centre should come out clean. Allow the cycle to complete, if required. Retest, extending baking time if needed.

When the cake is cooked, switch off the machine. Using oven gloves, carefully remove the pan. Allow the cake to cool in the tin for 10 minutes before turning out onto a wire rack to cool completely.

Tip
Barley malt syrup is available from health food shops. If you cannot find it, substitute 75g/3oz malt extract and 75g/3oz golden syrup.

Apple Cider Cake

Adding the sultanas.

A fabulous fat-free cake.

Place the cider, sultanas (or raisins) and apples in a saucepan and heat gently until just boiling. Simmer for 5 minutes and allow to cool.

Remove the bread pan from the machine. Add the cider mixture, followed by the eggs, flour and sugar.

Fit the bread pan in the machine, set the programme to the cake setting and press start. After 10 minutes scrape down the side of the tin with a rubber spatula. This will help ensure that the cake is fully mixed.

If the machine does not have a mixing facility, mix the cider mixture with the remaining ingredients, beating with a wooden spoon until well combined. Spoon the mixture into the tin and select the bake-only cycle for 50 minutes.

Check the cake mixture 10 minutes before the end of the cycle to see if it is cooked; a skewer inserted into the centre should come out clean. Allow the cycle to complete, if required. Retest, extending baking time if needed.

When the cake is cooked, switch off the machine. Using oven gloves, carefully remove the pan. Allow the cake to cool in the tin for 10 minutes before turning out onto a wire rack to cool completely.

Ingredients

150ml/5fl oz cider
100g/4oz sultanas, or raisins
2 medium eating apples, peeled, cored and chopped
225g/8oz wholemeal self-raising flour
1 tsp baking powder
75g/3oz light muscovado sugar
2 eggs

Honey Teacake

Pour the tea over the dried fruit.

Place the tea bags or tea in a measuring jug and fill to 200ml/7fl oz with boiling water. Allow the tea to steep for 5 minutes. Put the dried fruit in a mixing bowl. Pour or strain the tea over the fruit. Allow to stand for at least 2 hours. Strain the fruit.

Remove the bread pan from the machine. Add the soaked fruit and the remaining ingredients for the cake to the pan in the order listed.

Fit the bread pan in the machine, set the programme to the cake setting and press start. After 10 minutes scrape down the side of the tin with a rubber spatula. This will help to ensure that the cake is fully mixed.

If the machine does not have a mixing facility, beat together the honey, egg, oil, flour and baking powder with an electric whisk until smooth. Beat in the soaked fruit. Spoon the mixture into the tin and select the bake-only cycle for 50 minutes.

Check the cake mixture 10 minutes before the end of the cycle to see if it is cooked; a skewer inserted into the centre should come out clean. Allow the cycle to complete, if required. Retest, extending baking time if needed.

Drizzle chopped pecans, honey and sugar while the cake is still hot.

Ingredients
2 earl grey tea bags, or 2 tsp
  earl grey tea
225g/8oz mixed dried fruit
100g/4oz honey
1 egg
100g/4oz sunflower oil
225g/8oz self-raising flour
1 tsp baking powder

To complete:
2 tbsp honey
25g/1oz demerara sugar
25g/1oz chopped pecans
  (optional)

When the cake is cooked, switch off the machine. Using oven gloves, carefully remove the pan. Allow the cake to cool in the tin for 10 minutes before turning out onto a wire rack.

Heat the honey, sugar and chopped nuts, if using, in a small pan. Drizzle over the cooked cake while it is still hot. Cool completely, then serve cut into slices and buttered if liked.

Mincemeat Cake

An easy-to-make, moist family fruit cake.

Remove the bread pan from the machine. Add the ingredients for the cake to the pan in the order listed.

Fit the bread pan in the machine, set the programme to the cake setting and press start. After 10 minutes scrape down the side of the tin with a rubber spatula. This will help to ensure that the cake is fully mixed.

If the machine does not have a mixing facility, place all the ingredients, except the mincemeat, in a mixing bowl and beat with an electric whisk until combined. Beat in the mincemeat and spoon the mixture into the tin. Select the bake-only cycle for 50 minutes.

Check the cake mixture 10 minutes before the end of the cycle to see if it is cooked; a skewer inserted into the centre should come out clean. Allow the cycle to complete, if required. Retest, extending baking time if needed.

When the cake is cooked, switch off the machine. Using oven gloves, carefully remove the pan. Allow the cake to cool in the tin for 10 minutes before turning out onto a wire rack to cool completely.

Ingredients

300g/10½oz mincemeat
2 eggs
100g/4oz soft margarine or butter, softened
100g/4oz light muscovado sugar
250g/9oz self-raising flour
1 tsp baking powder

Adding sugar.

Adding mincemeat.

Date and Prune Cake

Adding the flour.

Check the cake mixture 10 minutes before the end of the cycle to see if it is cooked; a skewer inserted into the centre should come out clean. Allow the cycle to complete, if required. Retest, extending baking time if needed.

When the cake is cooked, switch off the machine. Using oven gloves, carefully remove the pan. Allow the cake to cool in the tin for 10 minutes before turning out onto a wire rack to cool completely.

Ingredients

3 eggs
6 tbsp milk
100g/4oz chopped dried dates
100g/4oz pitted no-soak, dried prunes, chopped
150g/5oz soft margarine or butter, softened
100g/4oz light muscovado sugar
250g/9oz self-raising flour
1 tsp baking powder

Remove the bread pan from the machine. Add the ingredients for the cake to the pan in the order listed.

Fit the bread pan in the machine, set the programme to the cake setting and press start. After 10 minutes scrape down the side of the tin with a rubber spatula. This will help to ensure that the cake is fully mixed. If the machine does not have a mixing facility, place all the ingredients (except the fruit) in a mixing bowl and beat with an electric whisk until combined. Beat in the fruit and spoon the mixture into the tin. Select the bake-only cycle for 50 minutes.

Dates and prunes.

Tropical Cake

Remove the bread pan from the machine. Add the ingredients for the cake to the pan in the order listed.

Fit the bread pan in the machine, set the programme to the cake setting and press start. After 10 minutes scrape down the side of

Adding eggs.

the tin with a rubber spatula. This will help to ensure that the cake is fully mixed.

If the machine does not have a mixing facility, place all the ingredients in a mixing bowl and beat with an electric whisk until combined. Spoon into the tin and select the bake only cycle for 50 minutes.

Check the cake mixture 10 minutes before the end of the cycle to see if it is cooked; a skewer inserted into the centre should come out clean. Allow the cycle to complete, if required. Retest, extending baking time if needed.

Ingredients

3 eggs

175g/6oz soft margarine or butter, softened

175g/6oz light muscovado sugar

150g/5oz self-raising flour

1 tsp baking powder

2 large ripe bananas, mashed

75g/3oz desiccated coconut

2 rings fresh or canned pineapple, chopped

When the cake is cooked, switch off the machine. Using oven gloves, carefully remove the pan. Allow the cake to cool in the tin for 10 minutes before turning out to cool completely.

Tip

If using canned pineapple, make sure that it is very well drained or the cake may become soggy.

Mash the banana with a fork.

Chocolate Fudge Cake

Adding baking powder.

Spread the filling and place the two halves of cake together to make a sandwich.

Ingredients

Cake:
100g/4oz plain chocolate
200ml/7fl oz milk
100g/4oz soft margarine or
    butter, softened
200g/7oz light muscovado
    sugar
2 eggs
225g/8oz self-raising flour
2 tbsp cocoa powder
1 tsp baking powder

Butter icing:
50g/2oz butter, softened
1 tbsp cocoa powder
100g/4oz icing sugar
50g/2oz plain chocolate,
    melted

This is a rich chocolate cake with a scrumptious chocolate butter cream. It is also delicious served hot with custard.

Place the milk and chocolate in a small saucepan and heat gently, stirring until the chocolate melts and combines with the milk.

Remove the bread pan from the machine. Add the chocolate milk and the remaining ingredients for the cake in the order listed.

Fit the bread pan in the machine, set the programme to the cake setting and press start. After 10 minutes scrape down the side of the tin with a rubber spatula. This will help to ensure that the cake is fully mixed.

If the machine does not have a mixing facility, place all the ingredients in a mixing bowl and beat with an electric whisk until smooth. Spoon the mixture into the tin and select the bake-only cycle for 50 minutes.

Check the cake mixture 10 minutes before the end of the cycle to see if it is cooked; it should be springy to the touch and a skewer inserted into the centre should come out clean. Allow the cycle to complete, if required. Retest, extending baking time if needed.

When the cake is cooked, switch off the machine. Using oven gloves, carefully remove the pan. Allow the cake to cool in the tin for 10 minutes

before turning out onto a wire rack to cool completely.

To make the icing, beat together the butter, cocoa and icing sugar until it is fluffy. Beat in the melted chocolate. Spread the chocolate mixture over the top of the cake or split the cake and use the chocolate mix as a filling.

Coffee and Walnut Cake

Adding the flour.

Beat in dissolved coffee.

Place the milk in a small saucepan and sprinkle the coffee granules over it. Heat gently until the coffee dissolves and allow to cool.

Remove the bread pan from the machine. Add the dissolved coffee and the remaining ingredients for the cake to the pan in the order listed.

Fit the bread pan in the machine, set the programme to the cake setting and press start. After 10 minutes scrape down the side of the tin with a rubber spatula. This will help to ensure that the cake is fully mixed.

If the machine does not have a mixing facility, place all the ingredients (except the walnuts) in a mixing bowl and beat with an electric whisk until smooth. Beat in the walnuts and spoon the mixture into the tin. Select the bake-only cycle for 50 minutes.

Check the cake mixture 10 minutes before the end of the cycle to see if it is cooked; it should be springy to the touch and a skewer inserted into the centre should come out clean. Allow the cycle to complete, if required. Retest, extending baking time if needed.

When the cake is cooked, switch off the machine. Using oven gloves, carefully remove the pan. Allow the cake to cool in the tin for 10 minutes before turning out onto a wire rack to cool completely.

Ingredients

Cake:
4 tbsp milk
2 tbsp instant coffee granules
3 eggs
175g/6oz soft margarine or butter, softened
175g/6oz golden caster sugar
225g/8oz self-raising flour
1 tsp baking powder
100g/4oz walnuts, chopped

To complete:
1 tbsp instant coffee granules
1 tbsp boiling water
100g/4oz butter, softened
225g/8oz icing sugar
walnut halves, to decorate

To complete, dissolve the coffee in the boiling water. Beat the butter until fluffy. Gradually beat in the icing sugar and then beat in the dissolved coffee. Spread the icing thickly over the top of the cake and decorate with walnut halves.

Sticky Walnut Cake

Spoon the syrup over the cake.

If the machine does not have a mixing facility, place all the ingredients in a mixing bowl and beat with an electric whisk until combined. Spoon into the tin and select the bake-only cycle for 50 minutes.

Check the cake mixture 10 minutes before the end of the cycle to see if it is cooked; a skewer

Ingredients
Cake:
250g/9oz walnuts
3 eggs
75g/3oz butter
75g/3oz golden caster sugar
75g/3oz plain flour
2 tsp baking powder
1 tsp ground cinnamon

To complete:
50g/2oz golden caster sugar
75ml/3floz water
2 tbsp brandy
grated zest and juice ½ lemon

This sticky, crumbly cake makes a fabulous dessert served with fresh fruit compote and a dollop of crème fraiche.

Place the walnuts in a food processor and process until very finely chopped. Remove the bread pan from the machine. Add the walnuts and the remaining ingredients for the cake to the pan in the order listed.

Fit the bread pan in the machine, set the programme to the cake setting and press start. After 10 minutes scrape down the side of the tin with a rubber spatula. This will help to ensure that the cake is fully mixed.

inserted into the centre should come out clean. Allow the cycle to complete, if required. Retest, extending baking time if needed.

When the cake is cooked, switch off the machine. Using oven gloves, carefully remove the pan. Allow the cake to cool completely in the pan.

To complete, carefully turn the cake out of the pan and place on a wire rack over a tray. Heat the sugar and water in a small pan, stirring until the sugar dissolves. Simmer gently for 5 minutes until syrupy. Stir in the brandy, lemon zest and juice.

Prick the cake all over with a skewer. Spoon the syrup over the cake so that it soaks in. Any spillages onto the tray can be respooned over the cake.

Carrot Cake

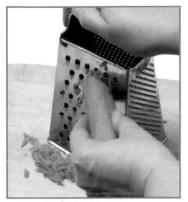

Grating the carrot.

A moist cake that keeps well, it can be served plain or topped with a creamy icing. Once iced, store in the refrigerator.

Remove the bread pan from the machine. Add the ingredients for the cake to the pan in the order listed.

Fit the bread pan in the machine, set the programme to the cake setting and press start. After 10 minutes scrape down the side of the tin with a rubber spatula. This will help to ensure that the cake is fully mixed.

If the machine does not have a mixing facility, place all the ingredients in a mixing bowl and beat with an electric whisk until combined. Spoon into the tin and select the bake-only cycle for 50 minutes.

Check the cake mixture 10 minutes before the end of the cycle to see if it is cooked; it should be springy to the touch and a skewer inserted into the centre should come out clean. Allow the cycle to complete, if required. Retest, extending baking time if needed.

When the cake is cooked, switch off the machine. Using oven gloves, carefully remove the pan. Allow the

Beat the cream cheese and orange juice together, then beat in the icing sugar.

Ingredients
Cake:
3 eggs
grated zest and juice
 ½ orange
225g/8oz carrots, grated
75g/3oz golden caster
 sugar
150g/5oz soft margarine or
 butter, softened
200g/7oz self-raising flour
1 tsp baking powder

Icing:
100g/4oz full-fat cream
 cheese
2 tsp orange juice
200g/7oz icing sugar

cake to cool in the tin for 10 minutes before turning out onto a wire rack to cool completely.

To make the icing, beat the cream cheese and orange juice together and then beat in the icing sugar. Spread over the top of the cake. Rough the icing with a knife or pattern with the prongs of a fork.

Ginger Cake

Adding the syrup.

Wonderful served as it is, or with a tangy lemon icing

Remove the bread pan from the machine. Add the ingredients for the cake to the pan in the order listed. Fit the bread pan in the machine, set the programme to the cake setting and press start. After 10 minutes scrape down the side of the tin with a rubber spatula. This will help to ensure that the cake is fully mixed.

If the machine does not have a mixing facility, place all ingredients in a mixing bowl and beat with an electric whisk until smooth. Spoon into the tin and select the bake-only cycle for 45 minutes.

Check the cake mixture 10 minutes before the end of the cycle to see if it is cooked; a skewer inserted into the centre should come out clean. Allow the cycle to complete, if required. Retest, extending baking time if needed.

When the cake is cooked, switch off the machine. Using oven gloves,

Ingredients
150ml/5fl oz milk
2 eggs
2 tbsp treacle
50g/2oz soft margarine or butter, softened
1 piece stem ginger, chopped
2 tbsp golden syrup, or syrup from stem ginger jar
50g/2oz golden caster sugar
300g/10½oz self-raising flour
2 tsp ground ginger
1 tsp baking powder

Icing:
175g/6oz icing sugar
2–3 tbsp lemon juice

Chopping ginger.

remove the pan. Allow cake to cool for 10 minutes before turning out onto a wire rack to cool completely.

To make a lemon icing, sift icing sugar into a mixing bowl. Stir in lemon juice to make a smooth icing. Spread over the top of the cake and allow to set before slicing.

JAMS

Many models now have a jam-making programme. They can be used to make small amounts of jam, usually 450–900g/1–2lb. These jams are often slightly lower in sugar than conventionally made jam and will, therefore, not keep as long. Use within 3 months unopened. Store in the refrigerator after opening and use within 4 weeks. Label your jars with the type of jam and date of making.

TIPS FOR SUCESSFUL JAM MAKING

• The time taken for the jam to reach setting point will depend on the ripeness of the fruit and the amount of pectin the fruit contains. Use extra bake time if required. Note: the extra time needed may be quite substantial.

• Do not open the lid while the machine is stirring the jam as it may splash. Jam gets very hot and will cause a nasty burn if splashed on the skin.

• Always use oven gloves when removing the pan from the machine. Place the pan on a trivet to protect the work surface.

• Remove the paddles with tongs before potting the jam in case they fall out and cause the jam to splash while pouring.

Raspberry and Pear Jam

Put all the ingredients into the bread pan and place in the machine. Select the jam setting and press start. Do not open the lid during mixing, as the jam may splash and hot jam will give a nasty burn.

While the jam is cooking, wash the jam jars, shake out the excess water and place them on a baking sheet. Put the jars in the oven at 150°C/300°F/gas 2 for 20 minutes to sterilize them.

Ingredients

400g/14oz frozen raspberries, thawed

250g/9oz firm pears, peeled, cored and chopped

350g/12oz jam sugar with added pectin

3 tbsp lemon juice

small knob butter

Peel, core and chop the pear.

Use oven gloves when pouring hot jam into jars.

When the jam cycle is complete, test the jam to see if it has reached setting point. Use the bake setting to extend the cooking time if needed.

Using oven gloves, carefully remove the pan from the machine. With a pair of tongs, remove the paddles from the machine. Carefully spoon or pour the jam into the warm jars. Seal with a wax disc and lid. Allow to cool. Label the jars.

Once open keep refrigerated.

Blackberry and Apple Jam

Ingredients
400g/14oz blackberries

250g/9oz Bramley cooking
  apples, peeled, cored and
  chopped

350g/12oz jam sugar with
  added pectin

3 tbsp lemon juice

1 tsp fennel seeds

small knob butter

Put all the ingredients in the bread pan and place in the machine. Select the jam setting and press start. Do not open the lid during mixing, as the jam may splash and hot jam will give a nasty burn.

Tip
Do not attempt to make jam in a bread machine unless your machine has a jam setting. Remember to take extra care when handling the hot jam.

While the jam is cooking, wash the jam jars, shake out the excess water and place them on a baking sheet. Put the jars in the oven at 150°C/300°F/gas 2 for 20 minutes to sterilize them.

When the jam cycle is complete, test the jam to see if it has reached setting point. Use the bake setting to extend the cooking time if needed.

Using oven gloves, carefully remove the pan from the machine. With a pair of tongs, remove the paddles from the machine. Carefully spoon or pour the jam into the warm jars. Seal with a wax disc and lid. Allow to cool. Label the jars.

Once open keep refrigerated.

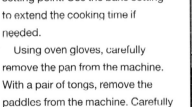

Adding sugar.

Sterilizing jars.

Strawberry Jam

Adding the fruit.

Ingredients
600g/1lb 3oz fresh or
   frozen strawberries,
   thawed if frozen
350g/12oz jam sugar with
   added pectin
3 tbsp lemon juice
small knob butter

You do not have to wait for summer to make this strawberry jam, as it can be made with frozen fruit.

Put all the ingredients into the bread pan and place in the machine. Select the jam setting and press start. Do not open the lid during mixing, as the jam may splash and hot jam will give a nasty burn.

While the jam is cooking, wash the jam jars, shake out the excess water and place them on a baking sheet. Put the jars in the oven at 150°C/300°F/gas 2 for 20 minutes to sterilize them.

When the jam cycle is complete, test the jam to see if it has reached setting point. Use the bake setting to extend the cooking time if needed.

Using oven gloves, carefully remove the pan from the machine. With a pair of tongs, remove the paddles from the machine. Carefully spoon or pour the jam into the warm jars. Seal with a wax disc and lid. Allow to cool. Label the jars.

Once open keep refrigerated.

Always use oven gloves.

Tip
Do not attempt to make jam in a bread machine unless your machine has a jam setting.

Remember to take extra care when handling the hot jam.

Plum Jam

Chopping and stoning the plums.

Ingredients
700g/1lb 8oz plums,
 stoned and chopped
350g/12oz jam sugar with
 added pectin
3 tbsp lemon juice
small knob butter

With a pair of tongs, remove the paddles from the machine. Carefully spoon or pour the jam into the warm jars. Seal with a wax disc and lid. Allow to cool. Label the jars.
Once open keep refrigerated.

Put all the ingredients into the bread pan and place in the machine. Select the jam setting and press start. Do not open the lid during mixing, as the jam may splash and hot jam will give a nasty burn.

While the jam is cooking, wash the jam jars, shake out the excess water and place on a baking sheet. Place the jars in the oven at 150°C/300°F/gas 2 for 20 minutes to sterilize them.

When the jam cycle is complete, test the jam to see if it has reached setting point. Use the bake setting to extend the cooking time if needed.

Using oven gloves, carefully remove the pan from the machine.

Tip
Do not attempt to make jam in a bread machine unless your machine has a jam setting.

Remember to take extra care when handling the hot jam.

Apricot and Orange Jam

Chop the apricots into quite small pieces because they will not break up during cooking.

Place the apricots in the bread pan. Heat the orange juice until almost boiling and pour over the apricots. Add the remaining ingredients to the pan.

Select the jam setting and press start. Do not open the lid during mixing, as the jam may splash and hot jam will give a nasty burn.

While the jam is cooking, wash the jam jars, shake out the excess water and place on a baking sheet. Place the jars in the oven at 150°C/300°F/gas 2 for 20 minutes to sterilize them.

When the jam cycle is complete, test the jam to see if it has reached setting point. Use the bake setting to extend the cooking time if needed.

Using oven gloves, carefully remove the pan from the machine. With a pair of tongs, remove the paddles from the machine. Carefully spoon or pour the jam into the warm jars. Seal with a wax disc and lid. Allow to cool. Label the jars.

Once open keep refrigerated.

Ingredients

350g/12oz no-soak, dried apricots, chopped
300ml/10½fl oz orange juice
300g/10½oz jam sugar with added pectin
juice of 1 lemon

Tip

Do not attempt to make jam in a bread machine unless your machine has a jam setting.

Remember to take extra care when handling the hot jam.

Chopping apricots.

Apple Mint Jelly

Chopping the mint.

Ingredients
600ml/1pt clear apple juice
1½ tbsp cider vinegar
400g/14oz jam sugar with
    added pectin
1 small handful mint leaves,
    chopped

A savoury jelly that is delicious served with lamb in place of the more traditional mint sauce.

Put all the ingredients, except the mint, into the bread pan and place in the machine. Select the jam setting and press start. Do not open the lid during mixing, as the jam may splash and hot jam will give a nasty burn.

While the jelly is cooking, wash the jam jars, shake out the excess water and place on a baking sheet. Place the jars in the oven at 150°C/ 300°F/gas 2 for 20 minutes to sterilize them.

When the jam cycle is complete, test the jelly to see if it has reached setting point. Use the bake setting to extend the cooking time if needed.

Using oven gloves, carefully remove the pan from the machine. With a pair of tongs, remove the paddles from the machine. Stir in the chopped mint. Carefully spoon or pour the jam into the warm jars. Seal with a wax disc and lid. Allow to cool. Label the jars.

Once open keep refrigerated.

Tip

Do not attempt to make jam in a bread machine unless your machine has a jam setting.

Remember to take extra care when handling the hot jam.

Summer Fruit Jam

The jam will wrinkle when cooled, if setting point is reached.

Remove paddles before potting.

Ingredients

400g/14oz mixed summer
   fruits, e.g. black currants,
   cherries, raspberries and
   strawberries
juice of ½ lemon
350g/12oz jam sugar with
   added pectin
small knob butter

A fruit jam that can also be made with frozen fruit.

Put all the ingredients into the bread pan and place in the machine. Select the jam setting and press start. Do not open the lid during mixing, as the jam may splash and hot jam will give a nasty burn.

While the jam is cooking, wash the jam jars, shake out the excess water and place on a baking sheet. Place the jars in the oven at 150°C/300°F/gas 2 for 20 minutes to sterilize them.

When the jam cycle is complete, test the jam to see if it has reached setting point. Use the bake setting to extend the cooking time if needed.

Using oven gloves, carefully remove the pan from the machine. With a pair of tongs, remove the paddles from the machine. Carefully spoon or pour the jam into the warm jars. Seal with a wax disc and lid. Allow to cool. Label the jars.

Once open keep refrigerated.

Tip

Do not attempt to make jam in a bread machine unless your machine has a jam setting.

Remember to take extra care when handling the hot jam.

Ginger Marmalade

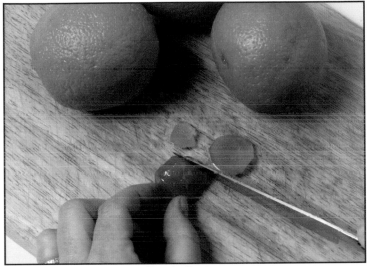

Chopping the ginger.

Ingredients

3 oranges

150–300ml/5-10fl oz
orange juice

350g/12oz jam sugar with
added pectin

1 tbsp chopped stem ginger

1 tbsp ginger juice from the
jar of stem ginger

A tangy, orange marmalade with a refreshing hint of ginger.

Using a potato peeler remove the peel from the oranges, taking care not to include the white pith. Shred the peel finely with a sharp knife. Squeeze the juice from the oranges and make up to 350ml/12fl oz orange juice.

Put all the ingredients into the bread pan and place in the machine. Select the jam setting and press start. Do not open the lid during mixing, as the jam may splash and hot jam will give a nasty burn.

While the jam is cooking, wash the jam jars, shake out the excess water and place on a baking sheet. Place the jars in the oven at 150°C/300°F/ gas 2 for 20 minutes to sterilize them.

When the jam cycle is complete, test the jam to see if it has reached setting point. Use the bake setting to extend the cooking time if needed.

Using oven gloves, carefully remove the pan from the machine. With a pair of tongs, remove the paddles from the machine. Carefully spoon or pour the jam into the warm jars. Seal with a wax disc and lid. Allow to cool. Label the jars.

Once open keep refrigerated.

Tip

Do not attempt to make jam in a bread machine unless your machine has a jam setting.

Remember to take extra care when handling the hot jam.

Citrus Marmalade

A delicious combination of citrus fruits makes this marmalade a winning formula.

Using a potato peeler remove the peel from the grapefruit, lemon and one of the oranges, taking care not to include the white pith. Shred the peel finely with a sharp knife. Squeeze the juice from the fruit and make up to 350ml/12floz with a little extra orange juice, if required.

Put all the ingredients into the bread pan and place in the machine.

Select the jam setting and press start. Do not open the lid during mixing, as the jam may splash and hot jam will give a nasty burn.

While the jam is cooking, wash the jam jars, shake out the excess water and place on a baking sheet. Place the jars in the oven at 150°C/300°F/gas 2 for 20 minutes to sterilize them.

When the jam cycle is complete, test the jam to see if it has reached setting point. Use the bake setting to extend the cooking time if needed.

Ingredients

1 grapefruit

2 oranges

1 lemon

extra orange juice if required

350g/12oz jam sugar with added pectin

Using oven gloves, carefully remove the pan from the machine. With a pair of tongs, remove the paddles from the machine. Carefully spoon or pour the jam into the warm jars. Seal with a wax disc and lid. Allow to cool. Label the jars.

Once open keep refrigerated.

Finely shred the peel.

Tip

Do not attempt to make jam in a bread machine unless your machine has a jam setting.

Remember to take extra care when handling the hot jam.